THE WITCH'S BOOK OF CANDLE MAGIC

Other Books by Cerridwen Greenleaf

The Magical Oracle Book

The Herbal Healing Handbook

Dark Moon Magic

Moon Spell Magic for Love

Mystical Crystals

The Magic of Crystals and Gems

Moon Spell Magic

The Witch's Guide to Ritual

THE WITCH'S BOOK OF CANDLE MAGIC

A Handbook of Candle Spells, Divination, Rituals, and Charms

CERRIDWEN GREENLEAF

mango
PUBLISHING GROUP

CORAL GABLES

Cover Design: Elina Diaz
Layout & Design: Megan Werner

For permission requests, please contact the publisher at:
Mango Publishing Group
2850 S Douglas Road, 4th Floor
Coral Gables, FL 33134 USA
info@mango.bz

For special orders, quantity sales, course adoptions and corporate sales, please email the publisher at sales@mango.bz. For trade and wholesale sales, please contact Ingram Publisher Services at customer.service@ingramcontent.com or +1.800.509.4887.

The Witch's Book of Candle Magic: A Handbook of Candle Spells, Divination, Rituals, and Charms

Library of Congress Cataloging-in-Publication number: 2022935524
ISBN: (p) 978-1-64250-867-3 (e) 978-1-64250-868-0
BISAC category code OCC026000, BODY, MIND & SPIRIT / Witchcraft

Printed in the United States of America

PLEASE TAKE NOTE:

ESSENTIALS OF
FIRE SAFETY

If you are going to delve into the techniques of magic using candles, it is key to approach the animating elemental force of Fire grounded in knowledge of and respect for it.

For starters, never leave a candle or other flame such as an incense charcoal unattended.

All containers used for candles or incense must be heat-tolerant (i.e., the container is not going to shatter or set other things on fire if its contents are very hot).

You may use:

- rock
- metal
- tempered glass (i.e., Pyrex)
- fired earthenware

Consider whether your container can be lined with a layer of sand thick enough to buffer heat, especially if you are using it with incense.

All containers used under candles must hold the liquid wax as it melts so it can't drip out. This keeps the surrounding area neat, and that way the flame can't follow the wax down and start a house fire.

You can shop for a suitable censer or thurible (incense burner) as well as beautiful candle holders at your favorite local five-and-dime, new age bookstores, and/or magical herb shops, such as my beloved San

Francisco emporia The Sword & The Rose or Scarlet Sage, two amazing shops that both also sell things online. Explore and find stores you love that you can turn to for many years to come.

Earthquakes: Consider what would happen with your burning candle(s) if an earthquake happened.

Of course, tremors occur more often in some geographic areas than others, but one can actually happen anywhere, so do not neglect caution in this regard. If you need to let a candle burn until done, really only a tile/porcelain bathtub (not fiberglass!) or a large braced-so-it-can't tumble metal bowl lined with sand will do. Those *can't* catch fire.

Note that incense charcoals, which are essential if you wish to burn fragrant magical resins like frankincense or copal, get *very* hot while burning and can *stay* hot for half an hour or so. Think carefully about what is holding the charcoal and also what is going to be underneath that, as well as how you can safely handle your incense burner if you need to move it. It may be useful to do a dry run using the charcoal before you utilize it in a magical working.

Take care and stay safe while working with the sacred flame.

CONTENTS

INTRODUCTION:

LIGHTING THE FLAME OF MAGIC:
HOW CANDLES CREATE ENCHANTMENT

C andles may be a simple tool, but they are also incredibly profound and can create powerful magic. They are a very old and enduring form of magic, and candle magic is still a mainstay of witchcraft today. It is used daily by folks in all different walks of life for peace of mind, respite, contemplation, and aromatherapeutic healing. In the age of COVID-19, many have found comfort and strength in the magical properties of candles.

Have you ever lit a candle just to observe the way it can transform a room? Try doing just that right now, preferably somewhere dark, and you will see exactly what I'm talking about. Take a moment to sit and observe, noticing how the darkness is transmuted by the candlelight. Watch how the flames flicker and cast shifting panes of light against the walls of your home, filling the atmosphere with the energy of magical light. The potential for transformation will become evident.

I don't know about you, but personally, I like to burn candles every night, 365 days a year, and take them with me when traveling, too. They imbue my personal space with positive energy and bring me a sense of calm.

Candles contain all four of the elemental energies:

- **Air:** Oxygen feeds and fans the candle flame
- **Earth:** The solid wax forms the candle
- **Water:** Melted wax is the fluid elemental state
- **Fire:** The flame sparks and blazes

Fire is the driving force behind candle magic. Fire is heat, and is the most visible form of energy. It is a powerful element, as it can transform and change the other elements. If you watch the flicker of your candle flame, the embers of your incense, or the blaze of your council fires, you will see a constant transmutation of matter. Fire has the ability to both excite and incite us, and fire is necessary to bring about change. Fire signs Aries, Leo, and Sagittarius are known for their strength and vibrancy. They can maintain this by employing their personal element of fire. Candle magic is a simple, powerful, and direct way you can invoke your native element of fire.

1

ALTAR CANDLES:
CREATING YOUR
POWER CENTER

An altar is a place of power—your personal power—where you can make magic. By building a stone shrine, altar, or power center in your home, you can create a sacred place for daily conjuring, rituals, and thinking. This will set the stage for you to focus your ideas and make them grow. Having a shrine in your home allows you to rid yourself of personal obstacles and invite friendly spirits into your space. Your shrine will spark your inner flame and bring daily renewal. The more use an altar gets, the more energy it builds, making your spells even more effective. It should be an expression of your deepest self, filled with artifacts that hold personal resonance. Allow your altar to be a work in progress that changes with the seasons and reflects your inner cycles.

I recommend starting with a flat surface, one at least two feet across each way for the four directions of the compass. Perhaps you have a favorite antique table, at once simple and ornate. I have set up my altar to face north, long believed to be the origin of primordial energy and associated with manifestation. North is also the direction of the hour of midnight, the "witching hour," and an altar set up facing north at midnight promises potent magic.

ALTAR BLESSING FOR PLENTY

Sit in a comfortable position in front of your altar and meditate. For this meditation, you should have an altar prepared that fills you with serenity. Light a green candle for prosperity, and reflect on the blessings you already have. What are you grateful for at this moment? There is powerful magic in recognizing all that you possess. Breathe steadily and deeply, inhaling and exhaling slowly for twenty minutes. Then chant:

> *Great Goddess, giver of all the fruits of this earth,*
> *of all bounty, beauty, and well-being,*
> *bless all who give and receive these gifts.*
> *I am made of sacred earth, purest water, sacred fire,*
> *and wildest wind.*
> *Blessing upon me. Blessing upon thee,*
> *Mother Earth and Sister Sky.*
> *So mote it be.*

ALTAR HERBS

Refer to this list whenever you are setting up your altar and setting your intention for ritual work. It is a concise guide to the enchanted realm of herbs, essences, plants, and plant properties.

Benzoin can be used for purification, prosperity, work success, mental acuity, and memory.

Camphor can be used for healing, divining the future, and curbing excess, especially romantic obsessions and a surfeit of sexuality.

Cinnamon refreshes and directs spirituality. It is also a protection herb and handy for healing, money, love, lust, personal power, and success with work and creative projects.

Clove is good for bringing money to you, for protection, for your love life, and for helping evade and deter negative energies.

Copal should be used for love and purification.

Frankincense is another spiritual essence that purifies and protects.

Lavender is a plant for happiness, peace, true love, long life, and chastity, and is an excellent purifier that aids with sleep.

Myrrh has been considered since ancient times to be deeply sacred. It aids personal spirituality, heals and protects, and can help ward off negative spirits and energies.

Nutmeg is a lucky herb that promotes good health and prosperity and encourages fidelity.

Patchouli stimulates and grounds while engendering both sensuality and fertility. It also supports personal wealth and security.

Peppermint is an herb of purification, healing, and love. It supports relaxation and sleep as it helps to increase psychic powers.

Rosemary is good for purification, protection, healing, relaxation, and intelligence. It attracts love and sensuality, helps with memory, and can keep you youthful.

Sage brings wisdom, purification, protection, health, and a long life. It can help make your wishes come true.

Sandalwood is a mystical, healing, protective essence that helps attract the objects of your hopes and desires and disperses negative energies and spirits.

Star Anise is a lucky herb that aids divination and psychism.

Tonka Bean brings courage and draws love and money.

Vanilla brings love and enriches your mental capacity.

Wood Aloe is good for dressing or anointing talismans and amulets you want to use for protection.

CRYSTAL SHRINES

Altar Crystals

The following is a comprehensive overview of different crystals and what their presence on your altar will mean.

CREATIVITY
Amazonite, aventurine, carnelian, chrysolite, chrysoprase, citrine, green tourmaline, malachite, yellow fluorite

INTUITION
Amethyst, azurite, celestite, lapis lazuli, moonstone, selenite, smoky quartz, sodalite, star sapphire, yellow calcite

LOVE
Amethyst, magnetite, rhodochrosite, rose quartz, twinned rock crystals

PROSPERITY
Bloodstone, carnelian, citrine, dendritic agate, diamond, garnet, hawk's-eye, moss agate, peridot, ruby, tiger's-eye, topaz, yellow sapphire

PROTECTION
Amber, Apache tear, chalcedony, citrine, green calcite, hematite, jade, jet, smoky quartz

SELF-ASSURANCE
Azurite, chalcedony, chrysocolla, green tourmaline, hematite, rutilated quartz, tiger's-eye

SERENITY
Amber, aventurine, blue jade, dioptase, Herkimer diamond, jasper, kunzite, moonstone, onyx, peridot, quartz, rhodonite

SUCCESS
Carnelian, obsidian, quartz, selenite, sodalite, topaz

VIGOR
Agate, aventurine, bloodstone, calcite, chalcedony, citrine, dioptase, emerald, garnet, orange calcite, ruby, topaz

WISDOM
Emerald, fluorite, Herkimer diamond, moldavite, serpentine, yellow calcite

Crystal Cleansing

Over time, you will doubtless adorn your sacred altar space with many beautiful crystals. Whenever you acquire a new crystal, you need to cleanse it. A new or waning moon is the optimal time to perform this cleansing. Gather these elemental energies:

- A candle for fire
- A cup of water
- Incense for air
- A bowl of salt

Pass your crystal through the scented smoke of the incense and say:

Inspired with the breath of air

Pass the crystal swiftly through the flame of the candle and say:

Burnished by fire

Sprinkle the crystal with water and say:

Purified by water

Dip the crystal into the bowl of salt and say:

Empowered by the earth

Hold the crystal before you with both hands and imagine an enveloping, warm white light purifying the tool. Now say:

Steeped in spirit and bright with light

Place the cleansed crystal upon your altar and say:

By craft made and by craft charged and changed,
This crystal I will use for the purpose of good in this world.
In the realm of the gods and goddesses,
I hereby consecrate this crystal.
Blessings to all, blessed be.

Creating Your Crystal Conjuring Shrine

Put your shrine together on a low table covered with a white scarf. Set rainbow candles in an arc and then add black and white candles. Prepare a heatproof bowl containing amber incense (good for creativity and healing), and place it in the center of the rainbow, surrounded by quartz.

Prosperity stones should be placed to the far left on the altar, in the money corner. Romance crystals should sit to the far right on the altar.

The rest of your altar should consist of personally meaningful symbols. They should reflect your spiritual aspirations. I keep fresh wildflowers in a vase, a statue of a goddess, abalone shells, a magnetite obelisk, and a rock-quartz crystal ball on my altar. You can use just about anything—photos of loved ones, religious images, and so forth. An obelisk or pyramid on your altar can be used for writing out desires and wishes.

With your altar, you can create a bridge between your outer and inner worlds. It can even be a place where you commune with the deepest and most hidden parts of yourself. An altar is where you can honor the rhythms of the season and the rhythms of your own life. An altar is a touchstone, a place to see the sacred and incorporate it into your life each and every day. It can be your special corner of the world where you can rest and connect with your spiritual center. Creating and augmenting your altar every day is one of the most soul-nourishing acts you can do.

Enchanting Your Jewelry with Candle Magic: Your Crystal Altar

Charging a gem or crystal imbues it with your intent. Upon charging your jewelry, you can use it in spell work or anytime you want to surround yourself with the magic you put into the gemstones. While picturing your truest wish and hope and what you ultimately want to achieve through this process, anoint a candle with an essential oil that most expresses your energy. Perhaps it is rose oil, or as in my case, amber.

Begin by lighting the candle and gazing into the flame. Then, place the piece of jewelry in front of the candle and say aloud, "Into this jewelry, I imbue my essence and the power of this blessed earth. This gem of great hue is charged until my magic is through. So mote it be!"

You can further empower the jewel by scratching your desire into the wax of the candle. Then, each time you burn the candle, place the gem before it and think upon your quest.

To enchant all of your jewelry, you need to create an altar for this express purpose. With a crystal-magic altar, you can prepare the way for letting crystal and gem magic into your life and focusing your desires and dreams. If you already have an altar in place, incorporate some of the following elements. The more you use your altar, the more powerful your spells will be.

Your gem-magic altar can be a low table, the top of a chest, or even a shelf. First, you must purify the space with smoke. Once you have cleansed the space, cover your altar with your favorite fabric; I recommend the color white. Place a candle in each corner. I prefer candles of many colors to represent the rainbow array of gems. Place gems and crystals of your choice around the candles. Rose quartz is a heart stone, and fluorite is a calming crystal, so these are good choices for grounding yourself, particularly if your altar is in your bedroom, as many are! Add to the altar fresh flowers, incense you simply love to smell, and any objects that have special meaning to you. Some folks place lovely shells or feathers they have found in their paths or on the beach, and others use imagery that is special, like a goddess statue or a star shape. The most important point is that your altar be pleasing to your eye and your sensibilities. You should feel that it represents the deepest aspects of you as a person.

Ideally, you will bless your altar on a new moon. Light the candles and incense, and say aloud:

Here burns happiness about me,
Peace and harmony are in abundance,
Here my happiness abounds.
Gems and jewels—these bones of the earth
Bring love, prosperity, health and mirth.
Be it ever thus that joy is the light
That here burns bright.
Blessed be!

You have now consecrated your altar. It will be here to ease your spirit anytime and will become your power source. Your altar connects you to the earth of which you and all gems and crystals are a part. Your altar will connect you to the crystal magic that has now entered your life. Whenever you want to add a dash of magic or a supernatural sparkle to a stone or piece of jewelry, you can place it on your altar for seven days. On the seventh day, wear the jewelry and bewitch everyone you encounter! Remember that your level of clarity and concentration will be reflected in the jewel's power.

Now, enjoy your sacred stones.

ALTARS FOR LOVE, WELLNESS, AND CREATIVITY

Light of Venus: A Shrine for Loving Magic

To create your altar, find a small table and drape it in richly colored, luxurious fabrics—perhaps red satin or a burgundy velvet scarf. Take one red and one pink candle and arrange them around a sweet-smelling incense such as amber, rose, or jasmine. Decorate your altar with tokens that represent love to you: a heart-shaped chunk of ruby glass, potpourri made with rose and amethyst, a photo of your lover. Fridays are the time for spelling love, right before dawn. Before you light your candles, anoint them with a love oil of your choice.

Scent your wrists, your throat, and your left breast over your heart with the same oil. Jasmine and rose have very powerful love vibrations to attract and charm a lover. If you desire sexual results, look into the flame of the red candle; if your desire is affection or flirtation, look at the pink candle instead. This simple spell, said aloud, will create loving magic:

> *Venus, cast your light on me,*
> *A goddess for today I'll be.*
> *A lover, strong and brave and true,*
> *I seek as a reflection of you.*

Finding the Sacred in Sensuality: Your Erotic Altar

To prepare for new relationships and deepen the expression of feeling and intensity in your love life, create a center from which to renew your romantic spirit. Here you can concentrate your energy, clarify your intentions, and make wishes come true. If you already have an altar, incorporate some special elements, such as red candles or red crystals, or anything associated with Venus, like copper or a seashell, to enhance your sex life. Your altar can sit on a low table, a big box, or any flat surface dedicated to magic. One friend of mine has her sex altar at the head of her bed. Begin by purifying the space with some smoke cleansing. Then cover your altar with a large red silk or silk-like fabric. Place two red candles at

the center of your altar, and then place a soul mate crystal—two crystals naturally fused together—at the far-right corner of the altar. These are widely available at metaphysical stores. Anoint your candles with jasmine and neroli oil. Also keep the incense you think is sexiest on your altar. Place fresh Casablanca lilies in a vase, and change them the minute they begin to fade. Lilies are heralded as exotic and erotic flowers, prized for their seductive scent.

FLAME OF PASSION ALTAR DEDICATION

Here at your magical power source, you can "sanctify your love." Collect your tools as well as meaningful symbols and erotic iconography and prepare for the sacred rituals of love.

Light the candles and incense and dab sensual essential oils between your breasts, near your heart. Speak aloud:

> *I light the flame of desire;*
> *I fan the flame of passion.*
> *Each candle I burn is a wish,*
> *and I come to you as a witch.*
> *My lust will never wane.*
> *I desire, and I will be desired.*
> *Harm to none, so mote it be.*

Blessings for Home and Harmony

On a low table or chest of your choosing, place a forest green scarf and a brown candle to represent your family. Add lovely objects that you have found around your home and garden: a special fallen leaf, ocean-carved driftwood, lacey dried lichen, smooth stones, or whatever your heart desires. It is of utmost importance to add a bouquet of wildflowers native to your area that you have gathered close to your home or purchased locally. This bouquet will help integrate your home into your neighborhood and the geographic area in which you live. If possible, add a sweetly scented sachet of potpourri made from your home kitchen garden: rosemary, lavender, thyme, and mint, all of which imbue your space with positive energy. Add personal mementos like photos or a locket with a photo of your spouse and children.

Burn your favorite essential oils, the ones that create an aura of instant comfort for you, such as vanilla, cinnamon, or sweet orange neroli in an oil lamp. Finally, anoint the brown candle while concentrating on peace and bliss surrounding your home. Chant:

> *Here burns happiness about me.*
> *Peace and harmony are in abundance,*
> *And here true bliss surrounds.*
> *From now on, disharmony is gone.*
> *This is a home of peace and blessings.*
> *Here sheer joy lives.*

This consecrated space will ease your spirits at any time. Your altar connects you to the earth of which you are a part.

Altar for Healing and Wellness

Find a pure white square of fabric to drape over your table, just touching the floor. Take two candles in matching holders and place them on the two farthest corners. Place your incense burner exactly in the middle. If you don't have a favorite incense yet, start with the ancient essence of frankincense. Select objects that appeal to you symbolically to place on your altar. I have a candlestick of purest amethyst crystal, my birthstone. When I gaze on the candle flame refracted through the beautiful purple gemstone, I feel the fire within me. This inculcates your altar with the magic that lives inside you, that lives inside all of us, and magnifies the ceremonial strength of your workspace. You should decorate your altar until it is utterly and completely pleasing to your eye. After you've been working spells for a bit, an energy field will radiate from your altar.

Fireplace altars today hearken back to this earliest custom. Home and hearth have primal appeal to the comfort of both body and soul. If you have a fireplace, it can become the very heart of your home. The fireplace is also one of the safest places for the ritual work of fire keeping. Sanctify your fireplace with a sprinkling of salt, and then set it up as an altar to the four seasons. Like the Vestal Virgins of old, you can keep a fire burning in a votive glass holder in the back of your fireplace and have an eternal flame. The fireplace can be your simplest altar and a reflection of the work of nature. If you don't have a real fire in your fireplace, you can place in it beautiful sacred objects—pretty rocks, feathers, seashells, glistening crystals, beautiful leaves, and anything representing the holiest aspects of the world around you. Let nature be your guide.

Your Prosperity Altar: Invoking Heavenly Bounties

You already know that your altar is the nexus of your magical powers, but it can also be a medium through which you give gifts to the Roman god of abundance, Jupiter, also known as Jove. Jupiter is a rain and thunder deity who also controls fertility. He will rain abundance down upon you if you gain his favor through ritual observance. His "jovial" qualities include leadership, jollity, generosity, expansiveness, and a royal manner. Your middle finger is your Jupiter finger, and you can also increase your fortunes by leaving a ring on your altar overnight and then placing it on the middle finger of either hand. Ideally, for the best result, it will be a green or gold stone such as peridot, tourmaline, or citrine.

If you can find a statue or bust of Jove, you should place this symbol on the right side of the altar accompanied by the image of an eagle, which is the ideal prosperity altar emblem, as the eagle is Jupiter's bird totem. The eagles of Rome and America are this royal bird of the king of gods. Lapis lazuli, the beautiful blue stone beloved of the Egyptians, is also sacred to Jupiter. The alchemical symbol for this stone is the astrological sign of Jupiter in reverse, and the blue of the lapis stone is associated with the blue of the sky god. You can increase your prosperity by remembering one of its most basic principles: *By giving, so shall you receive.*

To create a prosperity altar, consecrate the area with sea salt. Cover a low table with green and gold altar cloths or scarves and place matching candles on it. Each day, "recharge" your altar with an altar gift such as flowers, jade or other green crystals, golden flowers, scented amber resin, and coin-shaped pebbles. On any Thursday or new moon, light your candle at midnight and burn frankincense and myrrh incense. Make an offering of a golden fruit such as apples or peaches to Jupiter, and anoint your third eye with a corresponding essential oil such as myrrh, frankincense, apple, or peach. Pray aloud:

> *This offering I make as my blessing to all.*
> *Greatest of gods, Lord Jove of the sky.*
> *From you, all heavenly gifts do fall.*
> *Most generous of all, you never deny.*
> *To you, I am grateful, and so mote it be!*

Put the candle in a safe, fireproof place and let it burn all night. You will dream of your loved ones, including yourself, receiving a bounty of material and spiritual wealth.

Healthful Beginnings: An Altar of Healing and Protection

Creating a healing altar will safeguard your physical health and that of your loved ones. Set up your healing altar facing north.

To ensure healthful beginnings, find a pure white square of fabric to drape over your altar to make a *tabula rasa,* an altar equivalent to a "blank slate." Take two green candles; place them in green glass holders or votive glasses and position them in the two farthest corners of the altar. Place your incense burner in the center between the two candles and light the incense. Sandalwood, cinnamon, camphor, and frankincense are all powerful purification incenses that are perfect for the creation of a healing altar. Burn one or all of these purification essences to consecrate the space. Adorn your altar with objects that symbolize healing energy to you. You may perhaps choose a candleholder carved from a chunk of amethyst crystal, which contains healing properties; an abalone shell with the iridescent magic of the oceans; a small citrus plant bursting with the restorative power of vitamin C; or a bowl of curative salts from the sea.

These symbolic items, and any others that you select, will energize your altar with the magic that lives inside you. It is also important that the altar be pleasing to your eye and that it makes you feel good when you look at it so you want to spend time there each and every day. After you have been performing rituals there for a while, a positive healing energy field will radiate from your altar.

Conjuring Creativity: An Altar for the Imagination

Your personal altar is the ideal environment to incubate your ideas and can be a touchstone for daily conjuring and contemplation. By preparing your home and sparking your inner flames, you can clear away personal blocks and invite in friendly spirits who will aid you in personal pursuits, no matter what your line of work is.

On a low table or chest, place an orange or gold scarf and the following elements: yellow, orange, and gold candles for stimulating intelligence and clarity; bergamot oil for energy; and vanilla incense for mental power.

In an amber or clear glass bowl on the altar, place cloves and sage leaves. Next, add items that symbolize your personal creativity—perhaps a poem you wrote, a figure you sculpted, or a photograph you took of the altar.

Place benzoin, an herb for all-around mental strength and clarity, in your incense burner; it will bring inspiration from the psychic realm. Add any gifts from nature that inspire you—luminous shells, chunks of quartz, or feathers. Arrange your altar in a way that pleases you and stimulates your senses. Now, anoint the candle with bergamot essential oil while you meditate to clear your mind of any distractions. This is an essential step in opening the mental and spiritual space necessary to create, whether your intention is to create a ritual of your own design or an art project. Once you feel focused, light a sage leaf and wave it gently around so the cleansing smoke permeates your altar space. Light the anointed candles and the incense with a candle. Now set and speak your intention:

By my hand,
And by the blessing of the spirits,
The fire of my creativity
Burns bright,
Burns long,
Burns eternal.
Blessings to me and to all who create!

2

COLOR MAGIC:
THE SUPERNATURAL SPECTRUM

C andle magic and color magic are deeply intertwined. Ritual candles are chosen for their color correspondences and then carved and anointed with special oils chosen for their own special energy. Color is a deeply intuitive form of magic, and its effect on the human mind is widely recognized and is supported by an array of scientific studies. Think about color therapy, for example! The way that colors elicit a subconscious response from your brain is its own form of magic. Even skeptics will agree that different colors can change the energy of a room and alter your mood. You may also find that your favorite colors have something to do with your response to certain vibrational energies and or some things that you are unconsciously lacking in your life.

Color magic is incredibly simple and can be incorporated into all areas of your life, from your home decoration to all the items you adorn yourself with such as clothes, makeup, nail polish, and so forth! Creating a candle spell involving color can be as simple as applying the basic precepts of color magic: Have a clear picture of your desired outcome, and choose a candle in a color you feel is appropriate. Then, just light your candle and let it burn while you focus on your intention. Because color magic is so subjective, some differences of opinion do exist, and color itself is a magical system. You may study the following guide as you select your candles, but remember to let your instinct lead you above all else here.

WHITE

Because white contains the whole spectrum of colors, it can often be used as a catch-all candle color and can replace other candles in a spell if necessary. White is specifically associated with protection, purity, peace and harmony, truth, binding, sincerity, happiness, spirituality and the higher self, tranquility, and new beginnings. You might wish to use the power of a white candle either to get a fresh start to your day or to create a sense of calm throughout your space.

RED

Red is the color of passion! Signifying the lifeblood running through your veins, it can be used for protection, strength, health, energy, vigor, sex and sensuality, love, courage, and power. Red candles are fierce and bold, useful in love magic as well as to ignite your personal power and charisma. They will help you to overcome obstacles and become the most daring and confident version of yourself.

BLACK

Black candles are best known for their ability to absorb and destroy negativity. They have strong banishing powers, protecting you from any harm that might come your way in the form of negative energy or ill intentions. Black is also an excellent color to help you cope with fears of the unknown and is associated with acceptance, determination, grounding, security, release, endings, and grief.

BLUE

Blue represents emotion, honesty and trust, relaxation, and calm. It is a color that can bring peace to a restless heart and mind, and it is also associated with communication. There are a variety of shades of blue that have even more specific correlations and uses.

Light Blue

Light blue candles are associated with understanding, tranquility, healing, patience, happiness, and overcoming depression. They can offer insight and guidance and may help you to obtain clarity in confusing areas of your life.

Dark Blue

Darker shades of blue are useful for change and flexibility, and these hues are connected to the subconscious mind, psychic perception, and healing. Some use these candles for dreamwork and sleep. In comparison to light blue candles, dark blue candles tend to be more calming, while light blue can be a revitalizing color!

GREEN

Ah, green, the color of fertility and luck! Green is a great color to work with if you need a little financial boost as it is heavily associated with money and wealth, growth, prosperity, and employment, as well as all-around good luck. It is also related to beauty, youth, nature and earth magic, and success in gardening. Look to green for abundance and bountiful blessings!

GRAY

Gray is a neutral color, imbuing it with the potential for balance and stability. Gray represents impartiality, cancellation, and stalemates. It can protect from negative influences and is also excellent for meditation. Try incorporating a gray candle into your rituals when you are dealing with confusion or need to remain objective about a particular matter.

YELLOW

In need of a little pep in your step? Yellow is an energizing color that will bring you optimism and invigoration! Intelligence, charm, attraction, learning, inspiration, persuasion, confidence, divination, psychic power, wisdom, happiness, memory, and friendship are some of the meanings associated with the color yellow. Because yellow is the color of the sun, expect an awakening and stimulating effect from burning yellow candles.

BROWN

Brown is a color that connects us to the earth. Its magical uses are related to animals, home, family, grounding and stability, balance, strength, hard work, protection, and material things. Use this candle when you feel like you need to bring things back into perspective, or when you are casting a spell to protect your home.

PINK

Love, honor, fidelity, morality, and friendship are just a few of the associations with the color pink. It is a color for affection, affinity, romance, beauty, self-love, faith, and devotion. Pink also carries a feminine energy and can be a catalyst for reconciliation.

ORANGE

Orange is infused with the energies of adaptability, stimulation, attraction, encouragement, ambition, creativity, and success. It is also the color of justice, which makes it of great use in all legal matters. Orange is also the color of opportunity, so you may find an orange candle to be a useful tool when manifesting success in business, networking, or career changes.

PURPLE

Purple is a color symbolic of power, authority, healing, spirituality, ambition, and wisdom. Burning purple candles can be conducive to business progress, tension relief, meditation, exorcism, and deepening spiritual awareness.

CORRESPONDENCES OF THE DAYS OF THE WEEK

Sunday

The sun rules this day; use gold or red to get results with a boss, a promotion, or health, fame, and general success. Burning red candles on a Sunday can also help you to overcome fear and gain self-confidence.

Monday

The moon rules this day; use silver or orange to influence home, subordinates, and the emotions. Burning silver candles on Monday can promote inner peace.

Tuesday

Planet Mars rules Tuesday. Yellow is the color to use on this day to affect aggressions, sex, conflict, and confidence. To let go of anger, burn orange candles on Tuesday.

Wednesday

On Wednesday, Mercury rules. To manifest your will in the realms of communication, studying, and intelligence, burn green candles. For mental clarity, burn yellow candles.

Thursday

Thursday rules Jupiter. Burn blue candles for medical and legal issues, money, spirit, integrity, safety and security, or for a peaceful home.

Friday

Venus rules Friday; use indigo for matters relating to aesthetics and beauty, marriage, relationships, theater, art, music, or family. For physical well-being or success at work, burn green candles. For kindness and compassion, burn pink candles.

Saturday

Saturn rules over Saturday. Black is the color to burn to affect judgments, obstacles, and matters involving property. To overcome regret or guilt, burn white candles.

3

INTENTIONS:
USING CANDLES TO TAKE
CHARGE OF YOUR DESTINY

A s you may know well, Dear Reader, clarifying and focusing your intention is the ultimate key to success in any spellwork you perform. A clear intention is essential in order for you to channel your power and energy into attracting the outcome you desire. Beginning a ritual with a hazy or vague intent does not offer any direction for your personal power to go, and you may find you are more likely to either fail or be unsatisfied with the end results. Your intentions should be precise and attainable, and once you have mastered setting the perfect intention, your craft will be much more personal and have a more potent effect. This chapter will guide you through some strategies for intention setting and give you a framework to customize spells for your specific needs and desires.

HOW TO SET INTENTIONS FOR A RITUAL OF YOUR OWN DESIGN

When creating your own ritual, or performing any spellwork, for that matter, you must approach it with a definite concentration, so try to eliminate any distractions clogging up your sacred space. If a nagging worry is hovering in the back of your mind, you are not properly focused. You may even want to perfect an image of your intention and desire with creative visualization.

Part of your preparation should also include using ritual correspondences—the phase of the moon, the day of the week, the color of the candles you use, and much more. These things add to the depth and meaning of your ritual. Do you need to clear the energy and refresh your altar with some housecleaning? Do so and continue to focus on your intention as you create the foundation for a successful ceremony. While you are clearing energy in your space, you must also clear out the clutter in your mind. If you are in a state of inner chaos, the outcome will simply not measure up to your expectations. Perhaps it will help you relax if you listen to instrumental music or sacred chants. Conscious breathing or stretching will also help you make yourself ready for ritual. Constructing your inner temple is a marvelous process that can aid in your journey deep inside yourself.

Sit or lie down in a position that is comfortable enough to relax you, but not so comfortable as to allow you to drift off to sleep. As you breathe slowly and rhythmically, imagine a peaceful, beautiful place specific to your desires. It could be a white marble temple in a lovely sculpture garden under a still blue sky. It could be a mirror pool by a sacred grove. It must be pleasing to you, a place you can visit frequently in visualization. It can be any size or shape but should have certain aspects:

- **The Center:** Your inner temple should have a single center from which you can access all areas of the temple. This center space is a representation of your personal power center.

- **Reflective Surface:** Here is where you can take a look at yourself spiritually. The reflective surface can be a scrying mirror, a crystal ball, or even a pool of water. You can also use it to look at the past, present, and future.

- **Water:** Your inner temple can have any number of water sources, such as a waterfall, a well, a stream, or an ocean. Water represents our deepest levels of consciousness. Commune with your deepest self here.

- **Earth:** Here is where you ground yourself and create manifestation. Take stock of your deepest desires and goals here in a garden, forest, meadow, or wherever your imagination guides you.

Ideally, your inner temple has four doorways or gates, one each for the four directions and elements. Once you have created your ideal inner temple, you can now use it to perform ritual, as you have created permanent sacred space inside and outside this temple through visualization.

INTENTION CANDLE SPELL

Essential elements for this ritual are one candle of your favorite color, a candle holder, copal or cinnamon essential oil to represent spirituality, paper and pen, a ritual knife, and any visual aids you may require, such as photos, tarot cards, or a drawing of a deity you have made or found specifically for this ritual. Carefully select a representation of a deity with whom you feel a connection or who you believe will be benevolent toward your intention.

The "body" of the ritual refers to the act itself. It will further your intention if you carve related symbols and power words into your candle with the tip of your knife. Anoint the candle with the essential oil you have chosen. Dressing the candle with the oil from top to bottom adds the influence of attraction to your spell. Conversely, dressing the oil in the opposite direction, from bottom to top, adds banishing power to your spell.

Write your intention on the paper and then speak aloud:

> *Thus, I consecrate this candle in the name of* [insert the name of the deity here],
> *so this flame will burn brightly and light my way.*

Place the anointed candle in the candleholder, light it, and say:

> *Blessed candle, light of the Goddess,*
> *I burn this light of* [deity's name].
> *Hear my prayer, O* [name the deity]*, hear my need.*
> *Do so with all your grace*
> *and with magical speed.*

Now read your intention as you wrote it on the paper. Roll the paper into a scroll; then, using a few drops of the warm wax from your intention candle, seal your sacred statement. Place the paper on your altar or in a special place where it can be safe until your intention is realized.

Allow the candle to burn down completely in order to truly raise and release energy. It can be useful to use small candles or tea lights for spells that require candles to burn out completely, so you're not left sitting there for several hours. Once you have seen your spell come to a culmination, burn the written intention in a metal dish or in your fireplace in gratitude to the god or goddess who helped you. While other faiths may pray to God for help and favors, this differs in that you are helping yourself: you are taking action and setting your intention, not simply turning over all responsibility to a higher power.

CENTER YOURSELF WITH THE HELP OF A LITTLE CANDLE MAGIC

The best way to prepare for personal ritual is to center yourself. I call this "doing a readjustment," and I believe this is especially important in our overscheduled and busy world. Doing a readjustment helps pull you back into yourself and gets your priorities back on track. Only when you are truly centered can you do the true inner work of self-development that is at the core of ritual. Centering takes many forms. Experiment on your own to find out what works best for you. One excellent way to center is to light a candle and meditate on it. By focusing on the flame, you bring your being and awareness into focus. You can take this a step further with this spell for new insight into your life.

Step 1: Place one candle on your altar or "centering station." Light your favorite meditation incense. For me, *nag champa* immediately sanctifies any space and creates a sacred aura.

Step 2: Scratch your name into the candle with the tip of your knife. Next, scratch your hope onto the candle, either in words or other symbols.

Step 3: Light your candle and recite:

> *This candle burns for me.*
> *Here burns my hope for* [say what you are hoping for].
> *Here burns the flame of insight,*
> *may I see clearly in this new light.*

Sit with your eyes closed for a few minutes and picture yourself enacting your hopes and desires. You are setting your intention. Picture yourself in the company of people who inspire and teach you, those who bring insight and new light into your life. Let the candle burn down completely.

DRESSED TO THRILL: CHARGING YOUR JEWELRY WITH ENCHANTMENT

Before a special date night or big evening event, you can enhance your own energy field with jewelry magic. Charging a gem or crystal imbues it with your intent. Upon charging your jewelry, you can use it in spellwork or anytime you want to surround yourself with the magic you put into the gemstones. While picturing your truest wish and hope and what you ultimately want to achieve through this process, anoint a candle with an essential oil that most expresses your energy. Perhaps it is rose, or as in my case, amber.

Begin by lighting the candle and gazing into the flame. Then, place the piece of jewelry in front of the candle and say aloud,

> *Into this jewelry, I imbue my essence.*
> *In these stones lies the power of this blessed earth.*
> *This gem of great hue is charged until my magic is through.*
> *With harm to none, so mote it be!*

You can further empower the jewel by scratching your desire into the wax of the candle. Then, each time you burn the candle, place the gem before it and think upon your purpose.

4

ANOINTING AND DRESSING YOUR CANDLES: ESSENTIAL OILS, INCENSE, AND POTIONS

ressing your candles can add another layer of magical complexity to your spell work. When you dress a candle, you are attuning it to your specific intentions. There are many different tools and methods of doing so, from incorporating carvings and sigils to botanicals and scented oils: all of which will clarify your purpose and hone spiritual energy to enhance the power of your spells. Put simply, dressing is the process of anointing your candle with various oils and herbs. There are a number of essential oils that have magical uses and properties, hundreds even, so let this chapter be your introduction to the breadth of intricacy that dressing can bring to your candle work.

CHARGING YOUR CANDLES

"Charging" a candle means instilling it with magical intent. A candle that has been charged fills your personal space with the intention of all four elements.

Once you clarify your intention, cleanse your candles by passing them through the purifying smoke of a cedar bundle or some incense.

This stage is especially important if you have purchased new candles for your rituals from a store or metaphysical shop. Cleansing will rid the candles of any odd energies they may have absorbed from other places or people.

You can further charge your candle by carving a symbol into the wax. Warm the tip of your ritual knife using a lit match and carve your full intention into the candle wax. I like to use the thorn of a rose for this. You can use your ritual knife to write words, although many witches use symbols—a heart, a dollar sign, or a number, for example. As you engrave the appropriate magical words onto the candle, you are charging it with energy and your hope and purpose for this spell. Some highly successful examples of this I have used and witnessed in circle gatherings are: "Healing for my friend who is in the hospital; she will recover for renewed and increased health." "I get the raise I am asking for, and more!" "New true love enters my life in the coming season, blessed be."

Next, you should dress your candle with a specific oil. Every essential oil is imbued with a power that comes from the plants and flowers of which it is made. You can also use oils to anoint yourself at the crown of the head or at the third eye to increase mental clarity. By using the inherent powers of essential oils, you are increasing and doubling the energies by anointing both your tool—in this case, the candle—and yourself.

Essential oils are highly concentrated extracts of flowers, herbs, roots, or resins, sometimes diluted in a neutral base oil. Try to ensure you are using natural oils instead of manufactured, chemical-filled perfume oils; the synthetics lack any real energy. Also, approach oils with caution, and don't get them in your eyes. Clean cotton gloves are a good idea to keep in your kitchen for handling sensitive materials. You can avoid any mess and protect your magical tools by using oil droppers. While you are learning and studying, find a trusted herbalist or the wise sage at your local metaphysical shop; usually their years of experience offer much in the way of useful knowledge that will be to your advantage as you work with candles.

MAGICAL MEANINGS OF ESSENTIAL OILS FOR YOUR SPELLWORK

These essential oils are some excellent choices for anointing candles as well as yourself.

- **Astral Projection:** Jasmine, benzoin, cinnamon, sandalwood
- **Courage:** Geranium, black pepper, frankincense
- **Dispelling negative energy and spirits:** Basil, clove, copal, frankincense, juniper, myrrh, pine, peppermint, rosemary, yarrow, vervain
- **Divination:** Camphor, orange, clove
- **Enchantment:** Ginger, tangerine, amber, apple
- **Healing:** Bay, cedar wood, cinnamon, coriander, eucalyptus, juniper, lime, rose, sandalwood, spearmint
- **Joy:** Lavender, neroli, bergamot, vanilla
- **Love:** Apricot, basil, chamomile, clove, copal, coriander, rose geranium, jasmine, lemon, lime, neroli, rose, rosemary, ylang-ylang
- **Luck:** Orange, nutmeg, rose, vervain
- **Peace:** Lavender, chamomile
- **Prosperity:** Basil, clove, ginger, cinnamon, nutmeg, orange, oak, moss, patchouli, peppermint, pine, aloe
- **Protection:** Bay, anise, black pepper, cedar, clove, cypress, copal, eucalyptus, frankincense, rose geranium, lime, myrrh, lavender, juniper, sandalwood, vetiver
- **Sexuality:** Cardamom, lemongrass, amber, rose, clove, olive, patchouli

AN OIL BLEND FOR FRIENDSHIP

This blend of oils can be used for anointing candles and dabbing pulse points. It contains oils for the four directions, representing alliance, and will strengthen the bond between you and your friends. To create the blend, have a get-together with some of your best friends.

You will need the following essential oils:

- Lavender
- Rose
- Musk
- Honeysuckle

Mix these oils together in equal parts. Then, have each friend dip a forefinger into the oil mixture and stir clockwise. Raise the bowl of oil and pray together:

> *In the name of union,*
> *in the spirit of friendship,*
> *I bless this oil as I exalt the bonds that bring us together,*
> *and so it shall be.*

Complete the consecration by dabbing this magical potion on each other's pulse points: wrists, temples, throat, knees, elbows, over the heart, and behind the ears. Make sure you all leave with your own vial of this companionship essence, which you can use any time a spell requires it.

CARRIER OILS AND THEIR USES

A carrier oil is a vegetable oil that is used to dilute essential oils without diminishing the effect of the essence. It ensures that essential oils used topically are comfortable on the skin. Each essential oil carries specific vibrations that hold much curative power. These base oils support other ingredients, including essential oils, and can be a vessel for healing in and of themselves.

Apricot kernel oil, with its warmth and resilience, is especially good for women. Apricot protects love and nurtures women at every age and stage of life.

Avocado is thick, dense, and earthy, a powerful element in any love potion. It also is excellent for drawing forth money and is helpful in business and financial matters.

Borage oil brings a connection with the higher mind, as well as courage, a sense of honor, and the ability to cope with whatever life sends your way. It is said to encourage truth and resolution in legal and relationship problems. If you feel you are being deceived, turn to borage.

Evening primrose oil abets clairvoyance and paranormal gifts. It will help you to see clearly.

Grape-seed oil is regarded by some as the "food of the gods" because of the way it augments spiritual growth. This should be one of the oils that you turn to for anointing candles or any statuary of gods and goddesses before rituals.

Jojoba oil absorbs extremely well into the skin, bearing anything mixed into it along with it. It is also a remarkable anointing oil. It should be used in recipes that help to deal with depression and support perseverance in hardship.

Olive oil was named "liquid gold" by the ancient Greek poet Homer, and rightly so: It is about vitality, money, success, and joyfulness.

Sunflower oil is permeated with the energy of our sun and is powerful and life-giving. Use it when you desire rapid growth and amplification of positive energy.

Sweet almond is a gentle, all-purpose oil ready to increase the energy of other ingredients.

PREPARE YOUR OWN SANDALWOOD OIL

While vanilla and amber is perhaps my favorite oil combination, I have recently moved into a sandalwood oil phase and am delighting in its powers. Sandalwood oil, ruled by both the sun and the moon, is very suited for use in protection and healing. It can be used as a massage oil and is ideal for friendship magic in particular.

To prepare this oil, stir together six teaspoons of powdered sandalwood and two cups of a neutral oil, such as sesame or almond, in a glass bowl. Heat the mixture gently over a flame, taking care not to bring it to a boiling point. After cooling, place it in a colored glass jar and seal it securely.

Sandalwood oil can also be used to cast wishes for yourself and your loved ones through candle magic. Anoint a red candle (to spark love and devotion) with the oil and place it on your altar. Speak your desire aloud three times while lighting and gazing on the candle, and you are sure to receive what you ask for.

BEYOND THE ESSENTIALS: A TO Z OILS FOR CANDLE ENCHANTMENTS

Agrimony oil has been used since ancient times and is very highly regarded as an all-purpose healer for the body. Turn to agrimony for help with sleep. It is a protective herb which brings about a sense of well-being and ease. Remember agrimony essential oil for your wellness rituals.

Amber oil is derived from the resin of tree sap. You can tell by its delightful scent that it contains much magic and is excellent for love spells. Amber will ground and balance your personal energy; it is also beneficial for purification psychic shielding and protection.

Basil oil is used in making perfumes, as well as in aromatherapy. It is extracted from the leaves of the basil plant; far from only being a culinary herb, this oil serves to aid in alertness, lifts the mood, and as a bonus, repels insects. The scent of this splendid oil is often spicy, warm, and healing. A must for money magic.

Bergamot's origins trace to Southeast Asia, where it was prized for its spicy and floral scent. Bergamot oil is most often used to lift moods and alleviate stress. Bergamot is like liquid sunshine. Send anxiety packing with bergamot essential oil, which is also exceptional for house magic.

Black Pepper oil, derived from the common peppercorn, is an oil that promotes emotional wellness and relaxes the nervous system. Aside from the common usage of flavoring meals, black pepper oil can be administered topically for stimulating the senses and engendering courage. It is also a protectant and can help keep bad energy and bad people out of your home.

Caraway oil enables us to rise above the earthly plan and see life in spiritual terms. It strengthens mental alertness and enhances memory. Caraway essential oil will protect your aura and empower visionary dreams if you sprinkle a couple of drops on your pillowcase at night before sleep.

Cardamom oil has a rich and spicy scent and is ideal for anyone who wants to deepen their spirituality in magical workings. It has a strong feminine energy and brings out generosity and open-hearted love. If you want to have greater happiness in love, try cardamom in romance rituals.

Carnation oil comes from a sweet small flower yet offers steadiness and strength, and it is also a guardian essence. Carnation will uproot buried emotions and help you process them so you can renew and reset. Carnation will improve communication and open your mind and heart to new experiences. If someone has been ill, carnation oil will support the renewal of stamina as it helps release the weakness and sadness of sickness and eases the way to a return to joy.

Cinnamon oil is beloved for its strong earthy and spicy scent. It is excellent for prosperity and protection. When properly diluted, cinnamon oil also serves as a great topical oil and brings anti-aging properties that work by enhancing circulation beneath the skin. Cinnamon essential oil brings money and blessings.

Citronella is best known for keeping insects at bay, but it is a truly wonderful antidepressant that is uplifting and encouraging. The sharp aspect of the scent clears the mind, too. Using it in a steam or a diffuser will keep the energy of your home clean.

Clary Sage oil is as magical for your skin as it is for your spellwork. When applied topically, it stimulates the skin and circulation while it soothes the mind. It is a natural antidepressant; and as its name hints, it brings clarity. It has a distinctly earthy aroma. Clary sage also brings visions and can open up your psychic ability.

Coconut oil is a sweetly scented favorite. Originating in Southern and Central America, coconut oil's plethora of healthy fats are a great addition to anyone's skincare and overall health. It also boosts moods and energy wherever its scent can go. Coconut oil's happy perfume aids memory retention, balances emotions, and stimulates weight loss, and it is a base oil that support and blends with other oils seamlessly.

Coriander oil is a clearing essential oil that abets overall health. With a fresh and fragrant scent, coriander oil is also a great aphrodisiac!

Dill, commonly found in Southwest Asia, gained popularity in eighth century France when Charlemagne ordered its mass cultivation due to its powerful healing properties. This fresh and bright oil calms the body as it quiets nervousness and anxiety.

Eucalyptus oil comes from the leaf of the eucalyptus tree, native to Australia. Fresh and minty, eucalyptus oil carries medicinal, antiseptic, and pharmaceutical benefits. These powerful properties are most often released by adding a few drops of this oil into water. In eucalyptus oil, we have an all-purpose therapeutic for coughs, colds, respiratory ailments, and insect bites. If you start to feel cold symptoms, use five drops of eucalyptus oil in a hot bath or in a bowl prepared with boiling water for a head steam.

Fennel oil is native to Southern European lands and is made from the seeds. It is very stabilizing and will focus your mind and aid in difficult work or challenges. Fennel seed oil has a buoyantly spicy and slightly licorice-like smell that opens the mind and helps with understanding. In a steam or diffuser, this is a helpmate essential oil at work and for space clearing before spells and rituals,

Fir oil, also known as Balm of Gilead, comes from the balsam fir tree. It has been in use since ancient times and is associated with forest spirits and tree magic. Druids claimed it helped with shapeshifting. It is an awakening essential oil and rebalances the heart and mind.

Frankincense oil is an ancient essence that has long been considered precious. This earthy and woody oil is perfect for clearing blocked nasal passageways to promote better breathing. Native to regions of Northern Africa, its benefits can be obtained by inhaling or massaging at pressure points. It is prized for use in magical workings including the highest kinds of spiritual ritual work. It keeps evil away.

Geranium oil is extracted from the South African flowering plant *Pelargonium graveolens*, and its sweetly floral oil is a true anti-inflammatory. Geranium offers emotional stability and lifts mood as well as immunity.

Ginger is native to Southern China and is a favorite around the world for the taste of its sharp spice. Ginger essential oil is very much a protector and is believed to ward off ghosts and negative spirit energies. It will also spice up your love life and is good for romance rituals. Ginger is a money attractor and will draw wealth toward you.

Hyssop oil is native to the Mediterranean region and is rich in spiritual properties. With a minty smell, this oil can be used to purify and abet the release of grief, sadness, and depression. It is protective oil which can be used for space clearing after an upset or for peace in your home environment.

Juniper Berry oil has a feminine energy and is sacred to earth deities. This essential oil has a sweet and woody aroma that makes it a great addition to aromatherapy and as an anointing application. It also has a strong clearing property for use before spellwork.

Lavender oil is my number one essential oil because it is so versatile. It is a natural antibiotic, antiseptic, sedative, antidepressant, and topical treatment for scalds and burns, as well as a good detoxifier. Lavender promotes healing, and the lovely scent has a calming effect and is widely used in aromatherapy.

Lemongrass oil is calming and balancing with a protective energy. Native to Asia, lemongrass has long been used to repel negative spirits from entering the home. The sharp and bright citrus scent can lift up those who are feeling blue and in a rut. It is also a love attractor. Lemongrass essential oil can help with a fresh start in life.

Lime oil comes from the fruit of the citrus tree. Traditionally lime oil's bright and fresh aroma is great for clearing any blocked energy channels and releasing creativity, as well as dispelling melancholy.

Mandarin oil has been in use since twelfth-century China, where it was beloved for its divine citrus scent and applications as a medicinal for both body and mind. This richly fragrant oil brightens moods and emotions and alleviates stress and insomnia. Mandarin can help you reconnect with your inner child and the innocence of youth.

Mugwort has long been used in magical workings starting in Mesopotamia and expanding in Europe, Asia, and now the world. It is used by shamans for dreamwork and achieving new levels of consciousness. Mugwort is especially good for the mental plane as it helps overcome headaches and soothes anxiety for mental balance and calm.

Myrrh is another precious essential essence from pre-Biblical times and is prized for its warm and lightly musky smelling resin. Hailed for the considerable anti-inflammatory benefits it provides, it is great for reducing pain and calming blotchy skin. An excellent anointing oil for candles, for lamps, and for yourself, this will connect you to the sacred dimension.

Myrtle oil is pressed from the myrtle tree, which was dedicated to Aphrodite in Ancient Greece. This slightly sweet and camphor-scented oil contains balancing benefits. It can be used to increase mood quality, prevent allergies, and clarify and cleanse emotional blockages. Myrtle is marvelous for us in goddess rites.

Narcissus oil has roots in classical Greek mythology and is indeed a visionary essence. It takes you to the realm of imagination. If you want to have intense dreams to feed your creativity, narcissus can bring those to you. Use it in conjunction with more grounding essential oils so you can also attend to practical matters as you explore.

Neroli oil is extracted from the bitter orange tree, originally found in Egypt, Algeria, France, and Spain. This essence contains regenerative qualities, making it a perfect topical to alleviate upset skin and even reduce redness. It is a goddess oil with a gentle feminine energy that both lifts emotions and helps overcome fear and worry. It can be used to get messages from dreams as well as astral travel.

Nutmeg oil is a warm, spicy essential oil that is sweet and somewhat woody. It blends beautifully with other essential oils in the same spice family and strengthens the combination. Nutmeg is very lucky and is wonderful in money magic. It is also fortunate for love and instills loyalty in a relationship.

Oakmoss oil has an earthy energy to match the name and can ground you and remind you of what you are supposed to accomplish during your life. It is very uplifting and brings inspiration. Oakmoss essential oil is an attractor of abundance and is highly recommended for money spells. It is also associated with older women and any rituals of cronehood, and elder woman's wisdom should include oakmoss oil.

Peppermint oil is a wonderful therapeutic for headaches, skin irritations, and depression. It is not surprising that peppermint oil is regarded as one of the world's oldest medicines. It is first rate in money magic as well as healing work and can be useful in divination.

Pine oil is renowned for its familiar clean scent and will restore your spirit when you feel gloomy. This earthy and fresh-scented oil is very useful in house magic and is connected to longevity and nature spirits, especially those of the woodlands and farmlands.

Rose oil is a favorite for its warmly perfumed scent. It is distilled from rose petals and used primarily as a fragrance. Originating in the Southern Andes, rose oil is great for nourishing and hydrating the skin and will envelope you in a delightful and elevating aroma. Rose essential oil is very useful in love spells as well as in energy management.

Rosemary oil, a woody and sweet-smelling oil, is a healer to use for flu, coughs, headaches, depression, muscular stress, arthritis, rheumatism, fatigue, and forgetfulness. Rosemary oil is stimulating and will perk you up if you do a head steam with it. You can also put a couple of drops in the bath to help aches, pains, and sniffles go away. It is unusual in that it can both relax you and stimulate your mind. Rosemary has a very cleansing energy and can imbue your home with coziness and contentment.

Sage oil has been around for a very long time. Gaining popularity in the Middle Ages, this spicy and uplifting oil contains natural antidepressants, as well as antibacterial and stress reduction properties. It is great for aromatherapy to reduce the user's anxiety and clarify their conscience.

Spruce oil is alternatively referred to as Black Spruce. It's a woodsy and rich oil that can promote mental clarity for its user. It is also very grounding for when you feel scattered. This has long been used as a medicinal by Native Americans, who value the positive effects it provides to mind, body, and spirit. Smelling the scent in a mist or diffuser can aid breathing, bring relaxation, and help you sleep. You can use it in purification rituals as it is used in Native American traditions.

Star Anise oil derives from the commonly used spice and is prized for the power to prevent misfortunes. Strongly and pleasantly scented, star anise essential oil increases psychic power. It can also be used in love spells and can bring back a lost love. It can change your fortune in many directions.

Tangerine oil has a very bright aroma that is wonderfully rejuvenating and stimulates mental clarity. It can also be used to both support the immune system and boost moods at the same time. Tangerine essential oil will bring a happy heart and a clear mind.

Tea Tree oil has been used by aborigines in Australia for centuries and is a powerful antibacterial, antifungal, and antiseptic. It has a fresh camphor smell and is used for space clearing and energy management. It can rid your home of negative energy swiftly and can be used to ward off malevolent spirits. Use tea tree essential oil to clear out and reset vibrations after an illness.

Thyme oil is an old-time curative highly valued and widely used by the ancient Egyptians, Greeks, and Romans. It confers boldness and is also a restorative to anyone who has faced challenges or great loss. It is a favorite in greenwitchery and house magic as a protectant.

Valerian oil comes initially from Europe and Asia and engenders an overall feeling of relaxation in its user. It can be used to deter restlessness and promote a full night's rest and is a great and nurturing aroma for girls and women. Valerian is also an anointing oil and is said to bring luck to your endeavors. It was especially popular during medieval times, when it was regarded as a major healing herb for many maladies.

Vanilla oil is obtained from the bean of the same name and has one of the most comforting, heartening and sweet scents of all. It is very useful for cheering yourself up, or for cheering up anyone else who needs it. It is excellent in house magic to create a cozy and safe sanctuary and very useful in spellwork for love and romance. It raises your personal energy level and is good for imbuing your home with positive, pleasant energy. Vanilla also helps with mental focus.

Western Red Cedar oil has a woody, strong and refreshing aroma and is powerful for grounding. It can also be used in nature spells and working with forest and plant deities and energies. This essential oil promotes longevity and helps you to retain youthful looks and energy. If you want to connect with Mother Earth, use Western Red Cedar oil.

Yarrow oil is good for both body and mind and can help with anxiety, tension headaches, muscle aches, and restoring overall mental wellness. It has a cooling effect on both emotions and muscles. A very pretty plant, flowering stalks of yarrow were bundled together and hung on front doors to ward off any evil, including people. The oil brings courage and will make you lucky in love, and it can also heal a broken heart or spirit.

Ylang-ylang oil benefits both the mind and body. This richly perfumed essential oil is a mood booster, anti-inflammatory, and aphrodisiac. Ylang-ylang instills confidence and overcomes shyness and is exceptional in sensual spells and love charms.

APHRODITE'S OIL OF LOVE

This oil stimulates desire and prowess in men. For women, follow the same instructions, but instead of the ginseng and yohimbe (which are greatly stimulating to men), substitute pinches of saffron and ground dong quai (also known as angelica root), long honored in the orient as a tonic for females.

In a favorite bottle or jar, ideally red or pink, mix together the following recipe with a silver spoon:

- Five drops rosemary oil
- Five drops patchouli oil
- Ten drops yohimbe extract[1]
- A pinch powdered ginseng root
- Two tablespoons light sesame oil

You can use the oils on your fingers to anoint candles, or even to massage your lover's body.

---

1   *Available at most herbal and metaphysical supply stores.*

5

CANDLE SPELLS FOR PEACE OF MIND

During times of turmoil, candle spells can be an excellent tool for filling your mind, body, and soul with a sense of peace and calm. These are spells that I have come back to time and time again for their soothing power. Living through a global pandemic has often filled my spirit with disquiet and worry, as I'm sure it has for you as well, Dear Reader. In fact, it is during this very difficult time that many have for the first time been drawn to the magical arts in search of solace from all of the fear and pain that surrounds us. Let the spells in this chapter take you on a fulfilling journey toward the peace and tranquility you so deserve.

SIGIL SPELL FOR HOPE

Carving symbols onto your candles is a simple and profound way to deepen your magic. What symbols are meaningful to you? Certain crosses, vines, flowers, hieroglyphs, and many other images have deep magical associations, so you should feel free to delve in and experiment to find the symbols that work best for you in your spells. The term "sigils" is derived from the word seal. A sigil is a magical glyph or symbol that is used in ritual to deepen focus or intensify magical powers. Methods for devising sigils for spellwork include using the planetary glyphs of astrology, runes, Enochian tablets, letters, numbers, or even mystical cyphers such as hermetic crosses or kabalistic signs.

If you are like me and have the artistic skill of a toddler, you can simply carve hearts, suns, and stars into the sides of your pillar candles. Whenever I am feeling low or distressed, I cast the following sigil spell. I take a bright yellow pillar candle and carve a sun into the side. Then I light my candle and intone:

> *Sol, our star,*
> *bring your light*
> *which none can mar.*
> *Burn long and bright;*
> *keep bad news afar.*
> *Send negativity out of sight.*
> *So mote it be.*

I then meditate on the candle flame and just breathe in and envision sunnier days.

CANDLE CONSECRATION FOR PEACE AND LOVE

I have recently been making, burning, and giving away candles with the word "peace" written on them with crystals embedded in the soft candle wax as a way to spread love and goodwill. I highly recommend this practice, which you can do for yourself using crystals of your choice.

If possible, perform this spell during the night of the full moon for the greatest effect. Place your newly made peace candle on your altar and light some rose incense, which represents love and unity. Then, light the candle and chant:

I light this candle for hope,
I light this candle for love,
I light this candle for unity,
I light this candle for the good of all the world
that we should live in peace.
And so it shall be.

Sit in front of your altar and meditate, eyes closed, for a few minutes while visualizing peace in the world. Let the candle burn completely for full charging. Whenever the world around you feels chaotic, light this candle and meditate on a sense of peace enveloping you. Trust me, it will.

SILENCE YOUR INNER CRITIC: AN ENCOURAGEMENT SPELL

As the sun sets on a waning moon day, you can quiet the inner voices of negativity and criticism that get in the way of simple joy. When our moon ebbs, another grows forth, so this is an excellent opportunity to send away that naysayer inside of you and allow a more blissful, self-accepting side of yourself to shine through.

Gather together:

- 1 teaspoon of patchouli resin
- 1 teaspoon of rose hips
- 1 vanilla bean
- A charcoal disc
- 1 gray candle

Grind together a teaspoon each of patchouli, rose hips, and vanilla bean. Burn this resin-based mixture on a piece of charcoal on your altar (charcoal wafers are available from metaphysical stores in packs of ten). Light a gray candle for protection and meditate on the flame. As you meditate, think about how you sometimes doubt yourself and your instincts. Visualize clearing that from your mind. Think about your talents and your potential as you chant:

> *La Lune, Goddess of the Moon,*
> *as you may grow, so do I.*
> *Here, tonight, under your darkest light,*
> *I shall embrace all within me that is good and right,*
> *and bid goodbye to all the rest.*
> *Blessed be.*

Blow out the candle and cast it into a fireplace, outdoor firepot, or wherever it can be melted down completely and safely. You must completely destroy the candle, as it now contains the energy of your inner critic. You should feel lighter and brighter almost immediately!

SANDALWOOD STILLNESS: A GROUNDING SPELL

Sandalwood has been used for thousands of years in India. The woody, sweet smell clears your mind and reconnects you to the earth. This simple spell can actually be used every day as a prayer, or to prepare for meditation.

To begin, light a stick of sandalwood incense and "smudge" the area with the soothing smoke. Anoint a brown candle with sandalwood oil and light it.

To a scentless base oil, such as canola, olive, or light sesame oil, add:

- 6 drops sandalwood oil
- 2 drops lemon oil
- 2 drops amber oil

Warm this concoction in a clay oil lamp or carefully heat it on the stove over a very low flame. When it is warm to the touch, dip your left ring finger into the oil with care and anoint your "third eye," located in the center of your forehead, just above the eyes.

Sitting in the cross-legged lotus position, whisper three times:

> *Come to me clarity, come to me peace,*
> *come to me wisdom.*
> *come to me bliss.*
> *I sit in stillness, I sit in peace.*
> *As above, so below; and so it is.*

Meditate for twenty minutes, and then massage the warmed oil into your feet. You will be utterly and blissfully grounded now.

SERENITY OF THE SETTING SUN: A SPELL FOR MONDAYS

To clear energy and prepare for a week of calm clarity, find a blossom of your favorite white flower—iris, lily, rose—one that is truly beautiful to your eye. Monday's setting sun is the time for this spell, enacted immediately after the sun goes below the horizon. Anoint a white candle with clary sage oil and place it on your altar. Take your single white blossom and add that to your altar in a bowl of freshly drawn water. Place sage leaves on a glass dish in front of the lit candle and speak aloud:

> *This fire is pure; this flower is holy, this water is clear.*
> *These elements purify me.*
> *I walk in light with nothing in my way.*
> *My energy is pure, my spirit is holy, my being is clear.*
> *White light burns bright in me and all the words I say.*
> *So mote it be. And so it is.*

Burn the sage in the fire of the candle, then put in the glass dish where it can turn into ash, smudging your space with consecrating smoke as it burns. Stand in front of your altar and breathe in slowly and deeply six times. On the last, strongest exhalation, blow the candle out.

PRESENCE OF PEACE: CITRINE SPELL

To begin this comforting ritual, anoint a yellow candle with calming and uplifting bergamot oil, then light it to bring mental clarity. Place a yellow rose in a vase to the left of the candle. To the right, place a bowl containing at least two citrine or quartz crystals.

Next, you will need saffron water, which is made quite easily by simmering a single teaspoon of saffron from your cupboard in two quarts of distilled water. Let the saffron water cool to room temperature and pour it into the bowl of crystals. Put your hands together in prayer and dip them in the bowl. Touch your third eye in the center of your forehead, anointing yourself with the saffron water. Now, speak aloud:

> *Goddess great, fill me with your presence.*
> *This night, I am whole and at peace.*
> *Breathing in, breathing out, I feel your safe embrace.*
> *And so it is.*

BANISH YOUR WOES:
A THURSDAY CANDLE SPELL

We all need a health and happiness boost sometimes. This spell, aimed at supporting mental and emotional well-being, is best performed when the hardy spirit of Thor is in ascendance. On any Thursday, take a blue candle, dress it with cedar or bergamot oil, light it, and say nine times:

Fears and woes, I take respite;
worries and cares, you're out of sight.
Stronger and happier I will grow each day;
my soul has found its way.

If you do this for several weeks, your friends will notice as your health blooms and you simply beam with a bright, jolly, and renewed sense of self and well-being.

A RITE TO QUELL A RESTLESS MIND

One of the most powerful benefits you can gain from having a wand of your own is that it can focus and direct energy. And there are times when we all need that! I often experience "monkey mind," when my thoughts race around, preoccupied with the various anxieties and stressors of the day. For that reason, I have been creating more rituals and meditations to counteract a wandering mind, one of the woes of our over-busy world.

Needless to say, for the following spell you will need a wand. They are very commonly available from new age shops as well as online. If you find a fallen branch that appeals, you can sand it till it's nice and smooth and adorn it to your heart's content if you like by wrapping copper wire or other metals and attaching crystals. I recommend one large one at the end which you use as pointer, with which you can direct energy and draw circles, etc. This crystal can also be a marvelous tool for focusing your mind.

All you need for this spell is your wand and one candle corresponding to the color of your chosen crystal. For example, if it is an amethyst, pick a purple candle. Sit in a darkened room, light the candle, and speak this spell while holding your wand and looking through the crystal at the candle flame.

Intone these words:

> *My mind is bright and clear,*
> *I feel no worry or fear.*
> *Into this brilliant crystal, I peer.*
> *I call forth focused energy here.*
> *So mote it be.*

Depending on how anxious and worried your mental state might be, you may need to repeat the spell. When you begin to feel quiet and peaceful in mind and body, you can extinguish the candle and keep it at the ready when you next need to reel in your wandering mind.

PEACE OF MIND BLESSING BOWL

While a bowl is not a tool in and of itself, you can utilize bowls in your spellwork often, anytime you are inspired to do so. Three simple ingredients—a red rose, a pink candle, and water—can bestow a powerful blessing. The rose signifies beauty, potential, the sunny seasons, and love for yourself and others. The candle stands for the element of fire, the yellow flame of the rising sun in the east, harmony, higher intention, and the light of the soul. Water represents its own element, flow, the direction of the west, emotions, and cleansing. This ritual can be performed alone or with a group in which you pass the bowl around. Float the rose in a clear bowl of water, and light a pink candle beside the bowl. With your left hand, gently stir the water in the bowl and say:

> *I give myself life and health, refreshing water for my spirit.*
> *I give myself time to rest and space to grow.*
> *I am love. My heart is as big as the world.*
> *I am peace of mind. So be it, now and always.*

Keep the blessing bowl on your kitchen altar for three days and three nights. Dry the red rose and keep it on your nightstand or desk where it will always fill your heart with love.

DISPEL YOUR FEARS: A RITE FOR GOOD RIDDANCE

The world can overwhelm us at times with problems relating to work, illness, and all manner of problems that get in the way and want to stay. But these problems are *not* beyond your control! The ultimate best times to release bad luck and unwanted negative energies are immediately after a full moon or on any Friday the thirteenth.

For this spell, get yourself a big black candle, an obsidian sphere (or at least an obsidian crystal), a piece of white paper, a black ink pen, a cancellation stamp (readily available at any stationary store), and a big flat rock that is slightly concave in the center. Write on the paper what you wish to be freed from—this is your release request. Place the candle and the obsidian on the flat rock, and light the candle near an open window so the negative energy will leave your home. While the candle burns, intone:

> *Waning moon, most wise Cybele,*
> *from me this burden please dispel.*
> *Upon this night so clear and bright*
> *I release (my request) to the moon tonight.*

Bury the candle's base in your garden for thirteen minutes so that it stands in the earth as it burns. Take your stamp and mark the paper "cancelled." Put the candle out; fold the paper away from you and place it under the flat stone. Repeat this process for twelve more nights (thirteen total). On the last night, which should ideally be the beginning of the new moon phase, burn the paper and bury the candle, ashes of the paper, and flat rock far from your home. Give thanks to the moon for assisting you, and let go of your troubles.

CANDLE CALM SPELL

With this spell, you can create a week of blissful and composed calm! On a Monday evening during the waning moon, anoint a black or gray candle with violet essential oil. Place the candle on your altar beside a vase of fresh violets or other purple flowers. Sit in front of your altar as twilight begins, and when the sun is completely gone, light the candle and chant:

> *Care and woe, begone.*
> *I am the mountain, the river, the tree, the grass, and the moon.*
> *I receive my strength from Nature, and she is my center.*
> *Tomorrow and the next, all gladness will enter.*
> *Harm to none, only good.*

PERFUME OF PEACE OIL

This candle spell involves creating and consecrating a lovely oil you can use to instill a greater sense of peace within your mind and heart. Into a blue bottle, pour almond, soy, or any other unscented base oil, then add two drops each of neroli, chamomile, and Turkish rose essential oils. Shake the oils together to blend them. Next, take an orange and place it beside a lit lavender candle you have anointed with the potion. Chant aloud:

> *By my own hand, I made this balm.*
> *This divine essence contains my calm.*
> *By my own will, I made this charm;*
> *This precious potion protects from all harm.*
> *With harm to none and health to all.*
> *Blessed be.*

Anoint your pulse points—your wrists, throat, and heart, behind the ear lobes, and behind the knees—with the unguent and bask in a sea of calm.

Some other excellent oils for anxiety or a quick pick-me-up include frankincense, marjoram, hyssop, neroli (orange blossom), jasmine, nutmeg, and valerian. You can apply them directly to the skin or use them for dressing your candles!

6

CANDLE SPELLS FOR LOVE

L ove magic is one of the most popular and most potent forms of magic there is. The heart is a beautiful and powerful thing which can conquer any obstacle. And yet, love is also one of the aspects of life we get the most strung up on. Just listen to today's trending pop songs! Music is obsessed with love, with stories of blossoming feelings and decimating heartbreaks in every lyric. We are all caught up in a maze of emotion, trying to find a lasting connection in the midst of an uncertain world. Maybe that's what makes love magic so desired and so valuable!

Candle magic is a great way to ignite your inner lover and set your passion ablaze. This chapter is your introduction to a breadth of fantastic love spells and charms involving these waxy wonders. Keep turning the pages to find the answers to all your lovely wants and woes.

FLAME OF LOVE:
A NEW MOON CANDLE SPELL

If you are looking for love, perform this rite and you will soon find a lover to satisfy your needs. On the night of the next new moon, take two pieces of a pink or red crystal—rose quartz will do nicely—and place them on the floor in the center of your bedroom. If you are lucky enough to have two garnets, rough rubies, or pink tourmalines, by all means use two of those heart stones.

Light one pink and one red candle and speak this love and life-affirming chant:

> *Beautiful crystal I hold this night,*
> *flame with love for my delight.*
> *Goddess of Love, I ask of you*
> *guide me in the path that is true.*
> *Harm to none as love comes to me.*
> *This I ask and so it shall be.*

Now, make yourself ready!

SEALED IN FRIENDSHIP: SOUL MATE SPELL

If you are fortunate enough to have a soul mate, here is a special bit of sorcery to seal your fate together.

Take a white candle for purity, a red candle for deep affection, and two long-stemmed roses complete with thorns. Light the candles and hand each other a rose. Anoint the candles with honey to seal your bond with sweetness and rose essential oil for the sweet connection of friendship. Witchcraft was originally nurtured by groups of friends passing on herbal remedies and working spells together in covens.

Use red ink and a white feather to write a vow of friendship to each other on a piece of parchment. First, each of you should dip the feather in the red ink and write the name of the other on the paper. Both of you should then take a thorn from each other's rose, prick the ends of your pinkies on your left hands, and squeeze a drop of blood onto the paper atop each other's names. As each of you completes this, speak aloud:

Friend so dear,
friend so near,
our blood is mingled forever.
Our bond is true, together forever,
soul mate true blue.
So mote it be.

Now your friendship is consecrated, both in the eyes of the gods, and most importantly, to the two of you. Afterwards, bury the parchment, the roses, the candles, and the feather outside in a safe place you choose together. If you don't bury these things, you risk having your friendship interfered with.

COME-TO-ME LOVE SPELL

With so few opportunities to meet new people amidst the pandemic, it often feels like love is constantly slipping through our fingertips, just out of reach. And while this has certainly complicated our love lives, it also has made the interactions we do have so much more treasured. Perhaps you've experienced something like this; a stranger caught your eye at a Zoom poetry reading, you had a brief but meaningful moment in line for coffee, or perhaps you exchanged looks of longing across the aisle on your last grocery run. Whatever it was, you can't seem to shake that person from your mind. Now, your only hope is that chance will bring you together, right? Wrong!

To reconnect with this mystery person, try this surefire reunion spell. Take a man-shaped mandrake root (commonly available from magickal herbalists and metaphysical shops), or any statue, photograph, or figure of a man. Place it on your altar, surrounding the figure's base with red and pink rose petals, then add red and pink candles. Place two goblets of red wine beside this arrangement, and burn the candles every night for a week starting on Friday, Venus's Day. Sip from one of the goblets and recite:

Merry Stranger, friend of my heart,
merry may we meet again.
Hail, fair fellow, friend well met,
I share this wine and toast you,
as we merry meet and merry part
and merry meet again.

Make sure you look your best, as you will soon lock eyes again.

A LOVER'S TOUCH: SENSUALITY SPELL

I always giggle when I see over-the-counter sesame body oil in the pharmacy. Unknowingly, a woman will apply sesame oil and never understand why she feels so much sexier and attracts more glances her way. While that marketplace version will do in a pinch, a potion you've made yourself will be ten times as effective. You can use it as a skin softener or a massage oil.

In a cup of almond and sesame oil, add twenty drops of musk, sandalwood, or orange blossom oil. Shake well, then heat very slowly and carefully. I use a clay oil warmer with a votive candle beneath, but the stovetop will do, making sure the flame is set very low.

While you are tending the concoction, look into the candle or gas flame and whisper:

My lover's eyes are like the sun.
His body like the land.
His skin is soft as rain.
Tonight, we are one.

When the oil is a perfect temperature to your touch, pour it into a pink bowl and place it beside the bed. Tenderly undress your lover and gently lay him down on clean sheets or towels. With each caress, both of you will deepen your desire for each other. Prepare for a trance-like evening of magical lovemaking.

TRUE LOVE'S KISS: A DATE NIGHT RITUAL

As the world starts to heal, perhaps you are thinking about meeting that special someone for a face-to-face date for the first time in a very long while. And you, clever one, planned it on a new moon night. If this new moon happens to be in the signs of Taurus, Scorpio, Libra, or Pisces, you are *really* in for a treat tonight! Here is the last-minute preparation to guarantee you will have the time of your life. Gather the following ritual elements:

- 2 red candles
- Your favorite essential oil (mine is vamber, a concoction of equal parts vanilla and amber oils that makes me feel instantly erotic)
- Thorn of a rose

Take the two red candles and anoint them with your essential oil. Take the thorn and scratch your name on one candle and your lover's name on the other. Anoint yourself between your breasts and over your heart, and then speak these words aloud twice:

> *Tonight, under this moon's light,*
> *we will fall under each other's spell.*
> *Tonight, under these stars so bright,*
> *we will ignite a fire and never quell.*
> *With these lips, this mouth, and my art*
> *I will explore the sacred mysteries*
> *of the human heart.*

When your object of desire arrives, you should both get comfortable. At an opportune moment, ask your lover to light the two candles. Take his or her hand and place it over your heart, lean forward, and very gently kiss him or her. For this magic to blossom into full power, you should remain standing and only kiss, slowly and gently but with increasing intensity, for at least thirty minutes. The art of kissing begins with lips only, gently tickling, licking, and nibbling on your partner's lips before moving on to the fabulous French kiss.

SEEKING AND FINDING LOVE SPELL

On a small piece of paper, write the name of your would-be love in red ink and roll up the scroll. Anoint the paper with rose or amber essential oil. Tie the scroll with red threads, incanting one line of the following spell per knot:

> *One to seek my love, one to find my love,*
> *one to bring my love, one to bind my love,*
> *forever bound together as one, so mote it be.*
> *This charm is done.*

Keep the love scroll under a candleholder with red candles at the north corner of your altar until your will is done. Make sure of your desire; this spell is lasting.

SPELL FOR ATTRACTING NEW LOVE

To attract new love, two nights before the full moon, take a small pink votive candle and place it inside your cauldron or any large metal pot. Lay a rose and a bell beside the cauldron and your altar. Use either rose or apple blossom essential oil to anoint the candle's wick. For the next two nights, light the candle, cup it in your hands, and direct loving thoughts into its flame. On the night of the full moon, take a thorn from the rose and carve the name of your heart's desire into the candle's wax, reciting:

I will find true love.

Light the pink candle and ring the bell thrice, saying:

As this candle begins to burn, a lover true will I earn.
As this flame burns ever higher, I will feel my lover's fire.

Ring the bell three more times and watch the candle burn completely.

CRUSH THE CRUSH: A SPELL FOR UNREQUITED LOVE

To transform the object of your desire into your partner in passion, try this powerful attraction spell. Get together the following elements for this spell:

- Plain muslin cloth
- Dried sage
- 1 pink seven-day candle
- Red thread and needle or stapler

Take the plain muslin and cut it into two heart shapes of the same size. Sew (or staple, if you are in a hurry) the two hearts together, leaving a hole so you can stuff it with dried sage. Then sew it shut, and either write, or if you are really crafty, *embroider* the name of the object of your affections onto the muslin heart. Put it on your altar.

Each night at midnight, the witching hour, light the pink candle for thirty minutes beside the heart sachet and say aloud three times:

To [crush's name] *I offer affection.*
To [crush's name] *I offer attention.*
To [crush's name] *I offer joy.*
And in return, I shall have the same.
So mote it be.

Now, your crush will turn their attention toward you and be ready to return your affection.

GARDENIA RITUAL FOR LOVE AND ECSTASY

Tantra, a greatly overused and gravely misunderstood term, comes from Sanskrit, and means "Ritual, Meditation, and Discipline." It involves a form of mutual worship of the Godhead (lingam) and the Goddesshead (yoni), in which divinity is achieved through simultaneous erotic and emotional union. This exquisite approach to deepening the love between you and your partner requires you to share mutually held intentions.

At the nearest greenhouse or floral show, buy as many gardenias as your purse will allow. Ten or twenty of these heavenly flowers will fill your bower with a sweet, seductive air. Place some of the flowers in crystal-clear bowls of water and some in a warm footbath, and scatter some petals in your bed. Undress and light a single gardenia-scented candle at the head of the bed. Crush some of the petals and rub them into your skin and hair, then chant this love spell:

From the soles of your feet to the holy lingam
to the hair that crowns you, I will worship you tonight.
Love and God, on this evening, I share my entire being in ecstasy.
So mote it be.

Wearing nothing but one of the priceless blossoms behind your left ear, greet your lover at the door. Sit him in the bower bed and worshipfully wash, dry, and anoint his feet. When the two of you make love, you will reach new heights of sustained passion and spiritual intensity.

LET YOUR LOVE BLOSSOM: YOUR MAGIC GARDEN

A great relationship can be cultivated, literally. By planting and carefully tending flowers that have special properties—like night-blooming jasmine for heightened sensuality, or lilies for lasting commitment—you can nurture your relationship. During a new moon in the Venus-ruled signs of Taurus or Libra, plant an assortment of flowers that will surround you with the beauty and energy of sweet devotion.

Before you place your hothouse posies or seeds into pots or flowerbeds, bless the ground with a prayer of health for your plants, yourself, and your relationships.

Light a black candle to absorb and dispel bad energy and place it in the middle of a circle you have drawn with a stick. Dip your hand into a clay bowl of water and sprinkle drops behind you and before you. Sing out:

> *Great spirit, I offer you this petition.*
> *Please cleanse this land—you are the greatest magician.*
> *With my hands, I will plant and sow.*
> *Here, a healing garden will now grow.*
> *Blessings to you and to the Guardians of the Earth.*

INVOKE YOUR INNER GODDESS

At the next full moon, make a vow, alone or with your partner, to bring forth all your inner erotic powers. Begin with a blissful bath in oil-scented water; this essential oil must be the one that makes you feel sexiest. For me, it is an equal mix of vanilla and amber; my vamber has never failed me. When I wear this unguent, I feel as if a cloud of sensuality surrounds me.

Sit in a darkened room, encircled by flickering jasmine, musk, or "vamber" candles. Raise a cup of jasmine tea or a glass of wine from a vintage that represents a lucky year for you, and speak this spell aloud:

> *Now I awaken the goddess in me.*
> *I surrender to love's power.*
> *Tonight, I will heat the night with my fire.*
> *As I drink this cup, my juices flower.*
> *I am alive! I am love! And so it is.*

You will radiate passion and be intensely drawn to your lover.

LOVER'S LURE:
AN ENCHANTMENT TO ENTICE

This conjuration utilizes the secret language of flowers to bring your ideal love into your life. With visualization and daily spell work, you can create the love of a lifetime, custom fit to your specifications. Gather up:

- 2 candles shaped like human figurines, or two pink candles
- Rosemary essential oil
- Rose essential oil
- 2 fresh roses in your favorite color

Any witchy five-and-dime will have candles shaped like human figures; they are usually red in color. Get one each shaped like a man and a woman (or whatever configuration suits your need) and place them on your altar. If you can't find these waxen figures, use two pink candles. Also take the two fresh roses and place them in a vase on your altar.

Rub rosemary essential oil on each candle, then do the same with rose oil. Rosemary is for remembrance, and rose is for sweetness and affection. Now light the candles and whisper:

> *Brother mine, brother fair,*
> *new friend of my heart,*
> *merry may we meet and merry may we greet again.*
> *I draw you with my art.*
> *One rose for you, one rose for me.*
> *And so it shall be.*

Substitute "Sister" for "Brother" if that suits your need.

Each night when you are going to sleep, you should visualize your meeting and what you will say. Each morning, take a moment to meditate on the roses on your altar. Sooner than you think, your love will appear. Mother Nature, one of the guises of the goddess, will take her course.

THE MAGIC OF MASSAGE

Set the stage for hands-on pleasure before you knead your lover's body into rapturous bliss. Start with your favorite music. I prefer Indian ragas because they seem to have a naturally sexy rhythm. Whether it is the sound of classical guitar, angelic harps, or an ambient electronic band from Iceland, it should relax and bring pleasure. Light pink, red, and brown candles to create a loving, sexual atmosphere that is strongly grounded. Kindle incense your lover has previously complimented, and lay out towels you have warmed and oils and lubricants you have also warmed. Turn up the heat a bit and turn down the lights to simply create a "spa" feeling for complete unwinding. I have some honey, goose feathers, and an edible raspberry-and-mint rub I like to share as well.

First undress your partner, very slowly and gently. If your partner is open-minded to pagan ways, you should speak this incantation in his or her presence. If not, it is your silent prayer:

> *I call on you, Pan,*
> *god of the woods, goat, man, and boy.*
> *I ask your blessing on this day of joy.*
> *I call on you, Venus, Goddess of this night,*
> *may we find new seasons of delight.*
> *What I want is here and now.*
> *And so it shall be.*

Start with warmed oil and give a classic massage while your partner relaxes face down on the bed or massage table. The basic principles of magical massage are rhythmic yet sensitive gliding strokes, gradually shifting to deeper strokes. Use your body weight for firmer pressure.

After relaxing your partner's back, legs, and feet, have him or her turn over. Massage the chest, arms, and hands. Then glide down to the legs, occasionally brushing the genitals with a light touch. After you finish the legs and feet, slide back up the body and very delicately brush the genitals in a teasing way. Draw the tease out as long as you can so the energy builds and grows. Now is the time to start shifting the focus to more explicitly erotic activities.

One of the most important tips for an amazing connection: Look your partner in the eye as you pleasure him or her. Locking the eyes and keeping them open during sex will open up new dimensions of gratification.

FIRE-OF-LOVE LETTERS

Love letters are an ancient art that always deepens intimacy. This spell combines candle magic with letter writing to hone the desire between you and your partner.

You will need:

- Special paper and ink
- Perfume
- Wax

Take a sheet of paper and write with an enchanted colored ink, which you can either make yourself with berry juice or buy at the nearest metaphysical five-and-dime. Perfume the letter with your signature scent or one your lover appreciates, like amber, vanilla, or ylang-ylang. Seal it with a wax you have also already scented with a drop of essential oil and, of course, with a kiss.

Before your love letter is delivered, light a candle anointed with your preferred scent and say:

> *Eros, speed my message on your wings of desire.*
> *Make my lover burn with love's fire.*

Make sure you send your letter with a proposal for a tryst, requesting your lover's RSVP.

SIMPLY MAGNETIC: ATTRACTION SPELL

This is the perfect spell of enchantment to use when you have met a special someone and you wish to enhance your personal charm and allure. With this invocation, you are sure to attract your heart's desire! You will need the following supplies:

- 1 red candle
- 1 pink candle

- Essential oil (Jasmine and rose have very powerful love vibrations to attract and charm a lover)

Stand before your altar with tokens representing love. Light the candles. Scent your wrists, your throat, and your left breast over your heart with the same oil.

If you desire sexual results, look into the flame of the red candle. If your desire is affection or flirtation, look at the pink candle instead. Said aloud, this spell creates loving energy:

Venus, cast light on me,
a Goddess today I'll be.
A lover, strong, brave, and true,
I seek as a reflection of you.

7

CANDLE SPELLS FOR PROSPERITY

In times of financial hardship, a little bit of prosperity magic can go a long way. Perhaps you are looking to dabble in candle magic to attract wealth or luck. Money and material success certainly motivate many individuals, and ritual can be quite conducive to bringing in newfound riches, but richness and prosperity involve much more than just the numbers in your bank account. You probably aren't going to invoke a wad of cash left on your doorstep left by a mystical patron. However, what these candle spells can do is transform you into a magnet for divine wealth and new relationships, jobs, and opportunities that will provide fulfillment for all of your physical and spiritual needs.

UNDER THE WAXING MOON: A SPELL TO BANISH BAD LUCK

Your altar is the heart center of your home, holding the energy of your sanctuary. Yet the world is constantly coming in and bringing harmful energy over your threshold—problems at the workplace, financial woes, or bad news about new virus mutations or the climate crisis. All this negativity wants to get in the way and stay. While you can't do anything about stock market crashes, the rate of inflation, or a coworker's divorce, do not allow this bad energy to cling to you. Instead, you can do something about it with a home-keeping spell. The best time to release any and all bad luck is on a Friday the 13th or during any waxing moon. As you know, Friday the 13th is considered a lucky day on the witch's calendar.

Get a big black candle and a black crystal, a piece of white paper, a black pen with black ink, and a cancellation stamp, readily available at any stationery store. Go into your backyard or a nearby park or woodland and find a flat rock that has a slightly concave surface.

Using the pen, write down on the white paper that which you want to rid yourself and your home of. This is your release request. Place the candle and the black crystal on the rock, and light the candle near an open window. As the negativity is released outside while the candle burns, intone:

> *Waxing moon, most wise Cybele,*
> *from me this burden please dispel.*
> *Upon this night so clear and bright*
> *I release ___ to the moon tonight.*

Go outside and place the rock altar on the ground and visualize a clear and peaceful home filled with only positivity as the candle burns for thirteen minutes. Stamp the paper with the cancel stamp. Snuff the candle, fold the paper away from your body, and place it under the rock. Speak your thanks to the moon for assisting you. If you have a truly serious issue at hand, repeat the process for thirteen nights and all will be vanquished.

WITCH'S WILLPOWER BREW: INVOKING THE ENERGY OF SUCCESS

On a Monday, or any day when you need to ready yourself for important events, meetings, or other high-pressure circumstances, set aside a half-hour of quiet time and brew up some willpower to help you in any creative endeavors. Light a white candle anointed with peppermint oil, and then light spicy incense such as cinnamon.

Take a sprig of mint, some warm milk, and a few cinnamon sticks and stir these together clockwise in a white mug. Say aloud:

> *Herb of menthe and spicy mead,*
> *today is the day I shall succeed*
> *in every word and every deed.*
> *So mote it be.*

Quaff the cup and "sit for a spell" with your eyes closed, envisioning your new horizons. Keep the cinnamon sticks on your altar as a symbol of the power of encouraging words.

THOR'S-DAY THURSDAY PROSPERITY POTION

This spell is truly marvelous for getting a new or better-paying job. You will get the best results on a new moon or full moon Thursday night, but any "Thor's Day" will do. Thursdays are named for Jupiter or Jove, originally Thor of Norse mythology, who represents joviality, expansion, and all things abundant.

To prepare yourself, begin by pouring a few drops of green apple or verbena essential oil into a vessel of hot water. Breathe in the steam deeply ten times, inhaling and exhaling deeply for cleansing. Light a single green candle. As you close your eyes, meditate on your true desires. What does personal prosperity mean to you? What do you really *need*? What do you most desire?

When you are clear about your answers, focus on the candle flame while intoning:

Here and now, my intention is set.
New luck will be mine and all needs will be met.
With harm to none and plenty for all, blessed be.

After your cleansing breath meditation, perform this tried-and-true
prosperity ritual to seal deals and bring new gainful employment and
fiscal abundance your way.

Light a yellow or metallic gold candle and light cinnamon incense to
go along with the candle. Place a piece of amethyst crystal by the candle
and incense, and repeat this incantation eight times while envisioning
yourself with perfect abundance at the perfect job:

I see the perfect place for me; I see a place of plenty.
Upon my heart's desire, I am set.
Prosperity comes to me now.

Place the vessel of water on your altar and let it cool. At midnight, pour
the prosperity potion on the roots of a nearby tree.

MAKE WAY THIS DAY: A SIMPLE
CLARITY INTONATION

Unless you are already a skilled practitioner of the magical arts, you may
well be unconsciously casting spells that throw obstacles in your path.
To clear the way to greater wealth and happiness, during the new moon,
pick one perfect white rose and sit in front of your altar with it. Light
a white candle with your eyes closed. Empty your mind and breathe
deeply. When you feel a buzzing at the crown of your head from inhaling
and exhaling so mindfully, stare into the flame and repeat seven times:

I am alive. I have power. It is real.

SUMMONED BY THE LIGHT OF THE NEW MOON: A NEW VOCATION SPELL

The new moon is an excellent time for ritual, especially when your focus is on bringing new things into your life, such as a job change. If you're seeking employment, try out the following ritual to manifest your desires. Get your supplies out:

- 2 green candles
- 2 white candles
- 2 gold candles
- 2 pieces of green jade or another green stone
- Cinnamon oil

Line up the candles, alternating the colors. Anoint each one with cinnamon oil, and rub a little oil on the stones, too. Start at one end and light each candle. As you light each one, repeat these words:

> *A new career is what's desired,*
> *I cast this spell so I'll be hired.*
> *By the light of this new moon,*
> *I need a new job soon.*

After all the candles are lit, take each stone and gently pass it through the flames, being careful of your fingers. Then hold the stones in your hands and visualize the type of job you want to get. After the spell, pocket the stones and carry them with you. You should have a new job by the next new moon.

DREAM JOB INCANTATION

Here is another spell that will attract new employment opportunities to you, and one that does not have the prerequisite of a particular moon phase. Light a gold candle and place it in a special place beside a chunk of shiny gold pyrite. Repeat this incantation eight times while holding the stone in your right hand. In your mind's eye, form an image of the job you most desire as you speak:

> *To see what the future holds,*
> *I must be bold.*
> *I see the perfect job for me;*
> *I see a place of plenty.*
> *Upon my heart's desire I am set;*
> *my new boss will never regret.*
> *This job will come to me now;*
> *harm to none, I vow.*
> *With harm to none, so mote it be.*

LET YOUR IMAGINATION PROSPER: A SPELL TO DISSOLVE CREATIVE BLOCKS

Is something getting in your way? Do you feel stalled out and overcome with procrastination? To overcome any blocks obstructing your creativity and productivity, you can dispel the negative energy by going for a walk in the nearest park. Find a round, flat rock, six to ten inches wide. This will become an altar supplied directly to you by Mother Nature, and it will have the purest energy. Begin by charging this stone on the full moon at your home altar. Light a white candle for purification, and then place your hand on the stone and chant three times:

Obstacles, take flight!
Goddess of Night, shine bright.
Moon of tonight, you give us delight.
Fill this stone with your light,
imbue it with all your magic and might,
surround it with your protective sight.
So mote it be.

Ideally, you'll want to perform this spell three times on three consecutive full moons before you begin drawing upon its energy. Like your altar, your stone will be a reservoir you can turn to any time you feel stuck or uninspired. This rock will emanate a quiet power you can draw from whenever you need.

PROSPEROUS POSSIBILITY ENCHANTMENT

Cinnamon, which you probably have a plentitude of in your kitchen cabinet, is a major source of prosperity and can even bring it about in a hurry. Here is a Jupiterian Thursday spell that will bring excellent opportunities your way.

Gather some cinnamon, both sticks and the powdered kind, and place it all on your altar. On a Thursday, light incense (preferably cinnamon) and walk through your house, wafting the delightfully sweet smoke into every room. Light two altar candles, one brown and one green. Gather yellow flowers such as daisies and adorn your altar with them. Stand in front of your earthen altar and consider the wonderful, full life you are going to enjoy. Pour the cinnamon spice and sticks into a bowl and pray aloud:

This humble spice I offer to the gods who provide all.
I am grateful for all I receive, no matter how small.
Now, I find I am in need,
blessings shall come now with great speed.

As above, so below,
the wisdom of the world shall freely flow.
To perfect possibility, I surrender.
And so it is. Blessed be to all.

CREATE YOUR OWN
LUCKY TALISMAN

If you are presenting your paintings to a curator or pitching your book to a publisher, you can wear a talisman of your own making to ensure a positive outcome. Many performers, athletes, and musicians have lucky pieces of clothing or some token that gives them the courage to put themselves forth in the best possible manner. I have lucky scarves that I have woven with golden thread and scented with my personally auspicious aroma of vamber.

To maximize the power of the talisman, consider the following suggestions, which I have used to great success. Keep in mind that this will work even better if you place the item on your altar to imbue it with the right energy. On a new moon night, or at least seven days before you perform or present your work, place your lucky scarf, glove, sock, or kerchief on your altar. Now, here is where a bit of candle magic comes in. Light a green, red, or blue candle, depending on your intention. Green is for abundance, red is for fame, and blue is for creative vision. Burn the candle for one hour every evening. When the big day comes, you will be ready.

For a speech, presentation, performance, or show, wear a red scarf. If you are preparing for a potentially lucrative deal, you must wear green. If you are trying to empower someone to see and share in your creative vision, blue is the right hue for you.

FOR WEALTH AND ABUNDANCE: GIVING GRATITUDE TO LORD JOVE

You should not be surprised to find another Thursday prosperity spell in this chapter, as this is the perfect day for invoking wealth and success! On any Thursday, or optimally, one occurring on a new moon, light your altar candle at midnight and burn frankincense and myrrh incense. Make an offering of a golden fruit such as apples or peaches to Jupiter, and anoint your third eye with a corresponding essential oil, such as myrrh, frankincense, apple, or peach.

Pray aloud:

> *This offering I make as my blessing to all.*
> *Greatest of gods, Lord Jove of the sky.*
> *From you, all heavenly gifts do fall.*
> *Most generous of all, you never deny.*
> *To you, I am grateful, and so mote it be!*

Put the candle in a safe, fireproof place such as a fireplace and let it burn all night. You will dream of your loved ones, including yourself, receiving a bounty of material and spiritual wealth.

TO ATTRACT BLESSINGS WE UNITE: A FULL MOON RITE

Here is a beautifully simple way to attract money and blessings to you and your circle. Be sure to pass on some of the good fortune that has shone on you in order to keep the flow of abundance in circulation. This ritual is most effective performed at midnight on a full moon. This ritual is intended to be performed in a group, so you will need to gather together companions with whom you are spiritually in tune. Ask each of the participants to bring a green candle with their name scratched into the wax. Find the biggest green candle you can get and light it at the stroke of midnight.

Ask each ritualist to step forward and say their name, lighting their candle from the large one. Pray aloud:

> *Holy Moon on this bright night!*
> *Now is the time for fortune to shine.*
> *Mother Moon, lend us your power*
> *in this midnight hour.*
> *Full moon bright, full moon's light,*
> *grant to us our wish tonight.*
> *Let abundance flow from this rite.*
> *With harm to none, so mote it be.*

Allow the candles to burn out on their own.

As they flicker under the full moon, gather the circle in a comfortable spot and talk about what you want to manifest in your lives. The more specific you are in the discussion, the better. This rite bears repeating every once in a while to renew its power.

LET YOUR LIGHT SHINE: A FIRST IMPRESSION SPELL

Are you going to an interview, meeting an artist's representative, or speaking to your new editor? Clearly, you will want to make the best impression when launching this important new relationship. To ensure that you start on the right footing, gather the following ingredients: oranges, an orange candle, a glass of orange juice, vanilla beans, vanilla incense, and pumpkin seeds. All of these contain the properties of sharpness, intelligence, and clarity.

In the first light of morning, light the orange candle and the vanilla incense. Eat half of the orange and five pumpkin seeds, drink the orange juice, and watch as the glow of sunshine fills the room with the radiant energy of the orange sun. Chant:

> *Sol, I bask in your bountiful rays,*
> *this and all days.*
> *As you shine, so shall I.*
> *So mote it be.*

Snuff out your candle and be prepared for a productive new relationship that will carry your work to new heights.

ANOINTED WITH ALMOND: CANDLE MAGIC TO ATTRACT WEALTH

Using almond oil is a simple way to attract money, and it can be employed to ease the discomfort of financial stress. Dress some green candles with a drop or two and burn them every day—this simple ritual will make a substantial difference. Almond oil works quickly because it is ruled by Mercury, the god of rapid change and communication, who operates in the realm of air.

While burning your almond-anointed candles, call upon Mercury:

> *Winged one, bring with you better days.*
> *Blessed be to all,*
> *and may they share*
> *in the bounty to come.*

While almond oil is a strong recommendation of mine, it is not the only oil you can use to enhance prosperity! Some floral essences that you can use to anoint your candles include:

- **Carnation** (a.k.a. Jove's flowers), which contain the strength of Jupiter and can facilitate healing, power, and fortune.
- **Chamomile**, which is said to bring success in gambling.
- **Cinnamon**, sacred to Venus and known to help bring good luck.
- **Honeysuckle**, which can bring psychic powers and creative inspiration, is also one of the most effective of all oils in attracting money.

GARDEN OF PROSPERITY: A RITUAL TO PLANT NEW BEGINNINGS IN YOUR LIFE

Nature is the ultimate creator. At a nearby gardening store or hardware store, get an assortment of seed packets to plant newness into your life. If your thumb is not the greenest, try a wildflower mix or poppies, which are extremely hardy and will grow quickly and spread, beautifying any area. They reseed themselves, which is a lovely bonus.

On a new moon morning, draw a square in your yard with a "found in nature" wand, a fallen branch. Apartment dwellers can use a planter on a deck or a big pot for this ritual. Each corner of the square needs a candle and a special stone. I get my stones at new age bookstores, which often have the shiny tumbled versions for as little as one dollar. Mark the corners as follows:

- Green candle and peridot or jade for creativity, prosperity, and growth
- Orange candle and jasper or onyx for clear thinking and highest consciousness
- Blue candle and turquoise or celestine for serenity, kindness, and a happy heart
- White candle and quartz or limestone for purification and safety

Repeat this chant as you light each candle:

> *Greatest Selene, I turn to you to help me renew,*
> *under this new moon and in this old earth.*
> *Blessings to you; blessings to me.*
> *Blessed be.*

Put the seeds under the soil with your fingers and tamp them down gently with your wand, the branch, which you should also stick in the ground at this time. Water your new moon garden and affirmative change will begin in your life that very day.

DECLARE YOUR RADIANCE AND CLAIM YOUR POTENTIAL

Throughout your practice, make sure to maintain a sense of personal abundance and acknowledge the great spirit within you. Be grateful for your body and for your health. Stand in front of a mirror, preferably naked, and drop all self-criticism. Concentrate on your real beauty and envelop yourself with unconditional self-love. Wrap your arms around yourself as you say:

> *In Her/His image, I too, am a Goddess/God.*
> *I walk in beauty; I am surrounded by love.*
> *Blessed be.*

Light three candles in your favorite color and scent. Sit in front of your altar and meditate on what will make you achieve your full potential.

Do you need to change your health habits? Do you need to open up your creativity? Do you need to revitalize with a vacation? Concentrate deeply, and choose three wishes to write down and place under your three candles. Every night for seven days, repeat this spell:

Today I arise.
This night I embrace my serenity, radiance, splendor, and wisdom.
Blessed be.

WRITE YOUR DESTINY: A WANING MOON SPELL

In days of yore, people often made their own inks, thus imbuing them with a deeply personal energy. They simply went to the side of the road and gathered blackberries or pokeberries from the vines that grew there. Often a bird flying overhead will supply a gift of volunteer vines best cultivated by a fence where they can climb, making berry-picking easier. When it comes to matters of the heart, contracts, legacy letters, and any document of real importance that you feel the need to make your mark upon, an artfully made ink can help you imbue your writings with power. This spell is best performed during the waning moon.

Gather the following for your ink recipe: a vial or small sealable bottle, dark red ink, 1/8th cup crushed berry juice, nine drops of burgundy wine, apple essential oil, and paper. You will also need one red candle.

Mix the juice, wine, and red ink in a small metal bowl. Carefully pour it into the vial and add one drop of the apple essence. Seal the bottle and shake gently.

Incant aloud:

By my hand, this spell is wrought.
With this ink, I will author my own destiny
and have the happy life and love I've sought.
So mote it be.

Now write the fate you envision for yourself in the near and far future using the enchantment ink and a feather for a pen. Let dry and seal it in an envelope, keeping it on your altar until the new moon phase. Then, by the light of a red candle, open the letter to yourself and read it aloud. After you have finished, burn the paper using the candle and scatter the ashes in your garden. By the next new moon, you will begin to reap the positive plans you invoked.

EARLY RISING RITUAL TO INSTILL YOUR DAY WITH BLESSINGS

How you begin your day can often set the tone for the entire day, and sometimes even longer. Therefore, it is incumbent upon us all to start the day out right! If you are not an early riser by nature, get up a half-hour earlier to instill enchantment into your morning. Gather up:

- 1 green candle
- 1 yellow candle
- 1 orange candle
- A sprig of fresh peppermint
- Peppermint essential oil
- Small dish for the plant

Immediately after you rise, place the items on your altar and dress the candles with the peppermint oil. Touch each candle with the plant for just a moment. Light the candles, then pick up the sprig with your left hand and hold it to your face so you can breathe in the fresh and elevating fragrance and speak aloud:

This is a blessed day, bright with possibilities.
Healing starts with this new day.
My body, mind, and heart are ready.

All good things are coming my way.
So mote it be.

Spend a few moments in contemplation and reflection and just
breathe in the essence of the mint plant and oils. Visualize good things
happening to you on this day and picture yourself brimming with energy
and exuberance.

SOWING SEEDS FOR FORTHCOMING BOUNTIES: A WAXING MOON INCANTATION

When the first narrow crescent of the waxing moon appears in the
twilight sky, place a green candle on your altar beside a white lily or
freesia. White flowers have the most intense aromas. Anoint the candle
with tuberose or rose oil. Take a handful of seeds, such as sunflower,
walnuts, or pistachios, still in their shells, and place them in front of
the candle.

Close your eyes and recite aloud:

Under this darkling moon,
in Eden fair, I walk through flowers
in the garden of my desires.
I light the flame of my mind,
I plant the seeds of things to come.

Meditate on what you wish to bring into manifestation while inhaling the
scents of the oil and flowers.

VESSEL OF ABUNDANCE

Having an attitude of gratitude lends a sense of satisfaction and generosity of spirit that will ease your way through the world. Here's a supremely easy way to give and receive by acknowledging what you already have.

Take the prettiest and biggest glass bowl, vase, or jar you can find, and place it on a hallway table or somewhere you pass every time you enter your house. Light a green candle beside it and chant to charge the candle with your intention:

> *Pot of gold, full of grace,*
> *bring good will and gifts to this place.*
> *So mote it be.*

Each time you come home, empty your pockets and purse of change. You will be amazed at how quickly the coins multiply. Whenever the vessel fills, take it to the bank and get the coins rolled. Take half and treat yourself to a spirit-raising indulgence, and then take the other half and give it to your favorite charity, perhaps a homeless shelter or a sanctuary for survivors of domestic violence. Just like power, generosity of spirit grows and returns to you tenfold. Be prepared for all forms of wealth to come your way.

BLESSING FOR A HAPPY AND PROSPEROUS HOME

When you or a friend move into a new home, place a wreath or bundle of dried hops and eucalyptus on the front door. Walk through the door, light your favorite incense and a brown candle, and lie down in the center of the front room. Whisper:

House of my body, I accept your shelter.
House of my spirit, I receive your blessings.
Home to my heart, I am open to joy.
And so it is. And so it shall be.

CANDLE SPELLS
FOR HEALING

These spells, Dear Reader, may be some of the most important ones you will ever perform in your practice. Healing is an ancient, earthen magic that was traditionally performed by village wise women. These women were herbalists, healers, and pioneers of folk medicine, drawing power from the earth and gathering wisdom to pass down through the generations, and the breadth of healing lore that these witches of old cultivated still informs the way we use healing magic today.

The rituals you will find in this chapter offer remedies to assuage illness, emotional distress, and heartbreak, as well as to promote good health and revitalize the spirit. Let this chapter take you on a beautiful journey of self-healing and fill you with love and generosity as you extend your healing magic to care for others in your life as well. This form of pure, selfless magic will surely nourish your spirit and that of all the people you encounter.

A RITUAL TO BANISH
YOUR ILLNESS

A friend of mine gets a cough every January like clockwork and has not quite figured out what causes it. In addition to some good commonsense health practices and extra attention to hydrating, herbal tea remedies, and healthy food with lots of rest, we created a banishing ritual that we performed outdoors. In current times, it could be performed remotely to good effect. Gather together:

- One gray candle
- Frankincense incense and burner
- Large fireproof dish
- Clary sage essential oil
- A three-foot length of thin jute or cotton rope
- A sharp knife
- Black tablecloth
- A bowl of water

Create a kind of simple outdoor altar on a table outside and cover it with the tablecloth. Now place the water, incense, candle, knife, and the rope on the altar.

The person who needs to release the illness or difficulty should raise their right hand and say aloud:

Here and now may this place
be consecrated before the spirits of earth,
air, fire, and water,
for we gather here
to perform a peaceful parting.
We hereby banish _____ [fill in the name of the illness or whatever needs to be banished]

Say the name of the person for whom the spell is being worked and light the candle and incense.

Now, take the rope and carefully cut it in half. Place the rope pieces on the incense and the incense charcoals in the fireproof dish and let the rope burn completely. Repeat the prayer and end with:

May all be well, may I be well.
Blessings to all and blessed be.

Put the candle and the incense out in the water bowl. Take the ashes from the rope and scatter them on a patch of earth nearby. Pour the water on the ashes, and you have now banished what you need to eliminate from your life.

MEDICINE FOR THE HEART SPELL

The Friday before the new moon—Venus's Day—is the perfect time to create a new opportunity and clear away relationship "baggage." Place a bowl of water on your altar. Light two rose-scented pink candles and a gardenia or vanilla-scented white candle. Burn amber incense in between the candles. Sprinkle salt on your altar cloth and ring a bell, then recite aloud:

Hurt and pain are banished this night;
fill this heart and home with light.

Ring the bell again. Toss the bowl of water out your front door, and all troubles of the heart should drain away.

SETTING DAILY INTENTIONS FOR HEALTH AND WELLNESS

To embark upon lifelong well-being, you will need to bring this awareness to every day of your life. Regular health rituals will go a long way toward this becoming a daily intention. Adorn your altar with fresh flowers and candles in colors that represent healing: yellow, red, and green. Every morning for seven days, light the candles and contemplate your future self in an optimal state of health, speaking this spell:

Today I arise on this glorious day
Under this rising sun, hear me say:
I will walk in wellness in every way
For body, mind, and soul, I pray.
Blessed be, and may it be so.

BLESSED BALM: DIY LOTION FOR EMOTIONAL HEALING

For a dreary day and a dark mood, use the strength of this olden unguent to release both mind and body. This desert plant produces a protective gel which works as both a sunscreen and a moisturizer. Combine the following oils with either four ounces of unscented body lotion, or two ounces of olive oil or sweet almond oil:

- 2 drops chamomile oil
- 2 drops neroli
- 15 drops aloe vera gel
- 6 drops rose oil

Shake the oils together and place in a corked pottery jar. Sit quietly in a room lit only by one blue candle after a bath and rub the balm gently into your skin. Pray aloud:

Work thy spell to heal and nurse.
Blessed balm, banish my pain.
Harm to none and health to all.

FLAME OF RESTORATION: A LONG-DISTANCE HEALING SPELL

As a healer, you will sometimes perform spells for those who are not present. You can set up another altar to represent the recipient of your magic or where you can have candles dedicated to the ailing one.

Begin by setting up two altar candles—one in the northeast and one in the northwest. Light them, then place three red candles on the east side of the altar and one orange candle on the west. The red candles stand for health and strength, while the orange candle lights the way for optimism and encouragement.

Light the orange candle and concentrate on attracting good health and good feeling for the sick. Next, light all three red candles and think of vitality and increasing the flow of energy while you recite:

> *Power of Light, Power of Love,*
> *the fire burns and we heal.*

SELF-LOVE HEALING RITE

This fire element ritual might become a regular practice for you, as it is fortifying to your spirit and feels simply wonderful. Gather the following:

- A large red pillar candle
- An orange
- Bergamot essential oil

Take the large pillar candle, anoint it with bergamot essential oil, and charge it with positivity toward yourself. Scratch your own name into it and write: "I love [your name]."

Light the candle and say four times:

> *I love me. I love* [your name].

Light the candle every night, and repeat this spell before bed and every morning when you arise. Your mood and sense of self will continue to grow in positivity.

REJUVENATE YOUR SPIRIT: A GARDEN WITCH'S SPELL

I advise any witchy gardener to have a rain barrel to make the most of stormy weather; you can use it to water your pots of herbs and your garden during sunnier days and dry spells. On the first day of seasonal rainfall, place a blue glass bowl outside as a water-catcher. Once it has filled with water, bring it inside and place on your altar beside a lit candle. Speak:

> *Water of life, gift from the sky,*
> *we bathe in newfound energy, making spirits fly!*

Dip your fingers in the water and touch your forehead. Meditate upon the healing work you and your garden can do, thanks to the nurturing rainfall. Pour the water into the ground of your garden, speaking the spell one last time.

CLAIM YOUR HEALTH: A CLARY SAGE INCANTATION

Here is a handy spell for physical well-being as well as a self-esteem boost. For this witchy approach to preventive medicine, take a green candle on a Friday, dress it with clary sage oil, and speak the following three times:

My health is mine, under this moon divine.
I choose to be well as in this healthy body I dwell.
No more pain and strife, vital breath of life.
Harm to none; health to me.
So mote it be.

CUPBOARD CURE: A RITUAL FOR CLEANSING AND VITALITY

Salts from the sea have been used to decontaminate the body by way of
ritual rubs since ancient times in the Mediterranean and Mesopotamia.
From Cleopatra to Bathsheba, these natural salts have been used to
exfoliate the skin and enhance circulation, vital to overall body health.
While there are wonderful imported Dead Sea salts readily available at
most bath and beauty stores, many witches prefer whipping up their own
healing beauty magic. To create your own cupboard cure, combine the
following:

- Three cups Epsom salts
- One tablespoon glycerin
- Four drops lemon essential oil
- Two drops jasmine oil
- Two drops vanilla
- One drop neroli oil (made from orange blossoms)

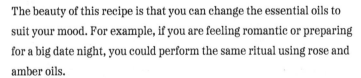

The beauty of this recipe is that you can change the essential oils to
suit your mood. For example, if you are feeling romantic or preparing
for a big date night, you could perform the same ritual using rose and
amber oils.

To prepare for your body glow session, light a white candle, step out
of your clothes and into your tub or shower, and hold the salts in the
palms of both hands, praying:

> *Aphrodite, in your wisdom, help me reflect your image;*
> *My body is a temple to thee, Goddess.*
> *Here, I worship today with my head and hands, heart and soul.*
> *Blessings to all, blessings to thee, blessed be me.*

Use the salts with a new loofah sponge and scrub yourself vigorously during the waning moon or new moon at midnight.

COMFORT IN COMPANY: A GROUP RITUAL TO PREPARE FOR SURGERY

Call your friends together before the surgery. The ritual can be at your home or any place that feels safe and secure. I highly recommend raising healing energy at the home of the person who is to undergo the surgery, as it will create an aura of restoration. Ask each person to bring something to comfort, reassure, and cure the celebrant: soup, fixings, a soothing eye pillow, sleep balm, a hand-knitted scarf for warmth, body lotion, herbal teas, books, or lavender-infused slippers are all wonderful gifts. Form a circle of care around the celebrant and light candles. Unscented soy candles are probably best for health reasons (and if a gift is scented, it is wise to check with the healing recipient whether that's okay in advance of the gathering). As you go around the circle, ask each person to give his or her gift of caring to the celebrant and say what it represents. As examples:

> *I give you this herbal tea mix so you can sip tea and draw from it*
> *healing and heat.*

> *I give you all my love and healing energy, and I know you will come*
> *back from the hospital healthier than ever before.*

The ritual continues until everyone has had a turn to speak and healing gifts and loving energy surround the celebrant. I suggest giving the celebrant hankies beforehand. It is completely up to the celebrant to say or do whatever he or she feels during the ritual. In many cases, they may say nothing due to the intensity of this event.

HEALING FOR YOUR LOVE LIFE: A NEW BEGINNING SPELL

This spell is excellent to use after a heartbreak or a trying time you may have had in your relationship with a current partner. In the event of a breakup, it may help you meet someone new; otherwise, it can heal hurts between you and your partner and bring on a new phase in your existing relationship. On a Monday morning before dawn, light one pink and one blue candle. Touch each candle with lily, freesia, or jasmine oil. Lay a lily on your altar, adding some fresh catnip if you can get it. Place a lapis lazuli stone in front of the lily, and a glass of water next to it atop a mirror. Chant:

> *Healing starts with new beginnings.*
> *My heart is open, I'm ready now.*
> *Goddess, you will show me how.*
> *So mote it be.*

Drink a cup of hot honeyed cinnamon tea that you have stirred counterclockwise with a cinnamon stick. Sprinkle the powdered version of this charismatic spice on the threshold of your front door and along your entry path. When the cinnamon powder is crushed underfoot, its regenerative powers will help you start a fresh chapter in your love life.

FROM EAST TO WEST: A SPELL FOR COLLECTIVE HEALING

The ultimate alchemy is to generate positive energy that spirals outward, improving everything in its path. I know of shamans and wise women who have dedicated their lives to doing good works, including some crones who practice in the ancient rainforest to protect the trees, and aborigines who spend their "dreamtime" repairing the earth.

You can contribute to universal peace and healing by burning a white candle, anointed with rose oil, on your altar during a waning moon on Saturday, which is Saturn's Day. Place a single white rose in water and lay a garlic clove beside some rose incense. Light the incense, then take an herb bundle, light the end, and pass the smoke over your altar to cleanse the space. Chant:

> *War and grief will come to an end*
> *as we walk the path of peace.*
> *Love thy neighbor as thy self,*
> *all we need is love.*
> *With harm to none, only understanding.*

TWO PATHS DIVERGE: A PARTING RITUAL FOR MUTUAL HEALING

Maintaining a healthy balance in your friendships is essential. Occasionally, a friendship takes on an unhealthy aspect and there is no choice but to leave it behind. Ideally you will perform this rite after you have discussed it with this person. It will be mutually healing if it can take place with both parties present, but as often as not, you will perform it alone. You will need a black candle for protection, a gray candle to help you keep a low profile, and frankincense incense. You will also need a sharp knife and a length of cord three feet long. Light the incense, and holding your right hand aloft, say:

> *May the place this night*
> *be consecrated before the spirits of earth,*
> *air, fire, and water,*
> *for we gather here to perform a peaceful*
> *parting of the ways.*

You and your former friend each light a candle.

> [Former friend's name] *and* [your name]
> *stand here today to let love and no rancor fill their hearts*
> *as they move separately through life.*
> *Blessings to all and blessed be.*

If you are so fortunate as to have the other person present, he or she repeats the above verse. Each of you takes the knife in turn and cuts the cord, representing the ties that bind you together as friends. If you are performing this ritual alone, get a photo of the other person and place it in the area where you are crafting your spell.

This is one of the more difficult rituals to perform, but it is invaluable nevertheless. I have noticed that when one person exits my life, especially for good and valid reasons, somebody new and wonderful comes in.

TRUTH WILL SET YOU FREE: A SPELL FOR SPIRITUAL HEALING AND GROWTH

If you find yourself in need of help resolving a problem or uncovering new resources within yourself, try the following tried-and-true rite.

Take a piece of plain white paper and a blue pen and have them at the ready.

On a Thursday, light some blue candles and chant the following affirmation:

> *Fears and doubt, begone from me!*
> *I have the courage to break free.*
> *I have the wisdom to know and the strength to grow.*
> *I call upon my inner guide to hear and see my truth.*

Repeat this four times while the candle burns. Embrace your intuition and trust it with all your heart. Now write down what comes into your mind with the blue pen. You may even feel tingling at the top of your head, which is a very good sign. Knowing the truth can sometimes be uncomfortable, but it is important as a guide for your life.

9

CANDLE DIVINATION: READING SIGNS AND SYMBOLS THROUGH SMOKE AND FIRE

Divination is a marvelous and exciting part of most any modern witch's practice, and it can take many different forms, from tarot reading to rune casting to scrying. It is also yet another aspect of witchcraft that frequently makes use of candle magic. The use of candles as an instrument of divining goes back thousands of years, spanning broadly across many different cultures. Candles are an excellent tool to illuminate the path ahead of you and assist you in navigating the future—enhancing your clairvoyance and opening your eyes to the intricacies and possibilities that your life journey holds.

NEW YEAR PROPHESIES: THE FEAST OF CARMENTALIA

On January 11, gather a group of women together. Ask them to bring pens and paper and offerings of fruit, flowers, or vegetables to the goddess Carmenta. Use these to build an altar, with the bounty placed around a black bowl filled with water that will be used as the scrying mirror. Place candles around the room and turn down the lights. Form a circle around the bowl and altar, and as each woman places her most special offering beside the bowl, she must speak aloud the name of her offering:

Pomegranate (or orange or lily, etc.), Goddess's herb,
perform for me enchantment superb.
You give us grain and bread.
Foretell for me the year ahead.

After placing the offering to Carmenta on the altar, each woman should kneel over the mirror and look upon the water. Some people may see images, but oftentimes the information comes as an impression, thought, or meditative reflection. People should only share their visions if they feel the need to do so, but do make a little time available for each woman in case she wishes to speak what she has seen.

After everyone has had a turn, everyone should chant and sing together:

Daughters under this sun,
sisters under this moon,
tonight, we receive your blessings.
Carmenta, goddess great and good—
we thank you for the year to come.

Now open the circle and sit in silence for at least ten minutes so that everyone present can record her impressions and visions from Carmenta in a journal or on the paper each woman brought. In years to come, if you and your circle of women decide to observe the Feast of Carmentalia annually, as I recommend, you can share and compare notes from prior years. This is a wonderful way to process the passages of your lives. Afterward, a feast is called for. The fruit and veggies from the altar should be consumed, and the flowers should decorate the dining table. Make sure to cleanse the space very well with incense smoke at the end of the evening, as remaining energies should scatter and not stay in the home. Water from the scrying bowl should be poured into the earth outside.

A MESSAGE FROM THE GUARDIANS: DARK MOON SPELL

This little spell will take you deep and far inside yourself. It will greatly empower you and instill in you a much deeper understanding of who you are and what you are here to do. Each of us is as individual as a snowflake, and our souls are imprinted with a stamp of specialness. The closer you get to the revelation of your soul's mission, the more you will know about why you are here, and even more important, what you are here to do. That is real magic.

The best time to perform this spell is during the dark of the moon, when the night sky is at its darkest.

Supplies:

- 1 votive candle
- Incense
- Pine essential oil
- Glass jar
- Compass

Go outside and find a solitary space in which you can cast a circle. Use the compass to find true north. When you feel comfortable and safe to begin, cast a circle of energy. Starting at the north point and moving clockwise or *sunwise*, acknowledge each of the Four Directions and call in the winter guardians. Stand in the center of the circle, and with your forefinger, anoint your candle with the essence of pine, a tree that stays strong, green, and alive all through the winter.

Place the candle in the glass jar and light it, setting both carefully and securely onto the ground. Then light the incense with the flame of the candle and stick it into the ground beside the votive candle. Breathe slowly and deeply; make yourself mindful that you are here in the darkest night, celebrating the sacred. As you breathe, look around at the majesty of nature and the world around you. Feel the ground beneath your feet. Listen to the silence around you.

Now, open your heart completely to the awesome power of the universe and the magic both inside and outside of you. Using the same forefinger, anoint your third eye, the chakric place above and between your eyes. With your eyes closed, speak aloud this rhyme of rime:

> *Sitting here beneath the moonless sky,*
> *I open my heart and wonder why*
> *I am here.*
> *Tonight, I will learn*
> *the reason why I yearn*
> *to serve the Goddess and the God.*
> *This night, I'll hear the reason*
> *I serve this darkest winter season.*
> *Guardians, I call on you now!*

Remain at the center of the circle and keep your eyes closed. You may hear an inner voice, or you may hear an outer voice right beside your ear. Listen calmly, staying centered with your two feet on the ground. You will know when it is time for you to close the circle and leave with your new message and mission. Thank the guardians as you seal the sacred space, being sure to leave everything exactly as you found it. Incense, jar, candles, and matches all leave with you.

When you return home, write the message on a slip of paper and place it on your altar, where it will be hidden from any eyes but yours. Place the candle, jar, and any remaining incense on your altar and burn it each Dark Moon night.

Final thought: You may also want to begin a special journal of your thoughts, inspirations, and actions regarding the message you received. You have now embarked on an exciting new phase of your life's journey. Your journal will help you as you make discovery after discovery. Your journal may evolve into a Book of Shadows, or it may one day become a book like this!

SYMBOLIC INSCRIPTIONS: A SPELL TO CONNECT WITH YOUR SUBCONSCIOUS

If you wish to make direct contact with your unconsciousness, here is a way to see through the veil between the two worlds and enter the recesses of your mind.

At any herbal store or metaphysical shop, obtain dry mugwort leaves and dried patchouli, as well as some wormwood if possible. The latter is a bit harder to come by, but worth the try. It is the active agent in absinthe.

Crumble any of these herbs between your hands until it is gently ground into an almost powdery consistency. Pour the herb into a baking pan. Make sure the crumbled herb dust is evenly spread over the surface of the pan.

Light yellow candles (from your creativity altar) and close your eyes. Take the forefinger of your left hand and touch the center of the pan. Run your finger back and forth in a completely random pattern—don't think, just rely on your instincts for two minutes. Open your eyes, look at the pattern you have drawn, and write down what the symbols and designs bring to mind. Also write down the thoughts you were having while you were "drawing." Some of my friends have found that they unconsciously wrote words, which they then used to start a poem or novel, or which generated an idea for a painting.

MYSTICAL MUGWORT SPELL: SHARPENING YOUR SECOND SIGHT

Honing your intuition will enhance every aspect of your life, and this spell, which can sharpen your sixth sense, is an excellent place to start. Gather together:

- 1 stick of vanilla incense
- Yellow candle
- Small jar or pouch of mugwort herb
- Small yellow citrine crystal
- Teaspoon of dried mugwort
- Ceramic bowl of hot water

Light the candle, and then light the stick of vanilla incense and place it in a fire-safe burner. Now place the single yellow flower in a vase to one side of the incense burner. Yellow symbolizes intelligence and mental clarity. On the other side, place a bowl containing a citrine crystal.

In your teakettle, boil two cups of freshly drawn water. Pour it in the ceramic bowl and add in the teaspoon of mugwort and stir. Once it has cooled completely, dip your fingers in the water and touch your "third eye" at the center of your forehead. Now speak aloud:

> *Diana, Goddess of the Moon,*
> *fill me with your presence divine.*
> *I seek your vision; lend me this boon.*
> *Greatest seer, may the second sight be mine.*
> *And so it is. And may it be soon.*

Mugwort has long been used in magical workings, starting in Mesopotamia and expanding to Europe, Asia, and now the world. It is used by seers and shamans for achieving new levels of consciousness. Mugwort is especially good for the mental plane and helps to overcome headaches and soothe anxiety for mental balance and calm. It will help you hone your psychic abilities, which will help and guide you through life.

10

MAJOR LIFE MOMENTS: CANDLE RITUALS AND GATHERINGS

Candle rituals are excellent for bringing you things like health, love, and prosperity, but they are also a beautiful tool to use in celebrating life! I love to gather together with my fellow witches and create magic together to rejoice in the beauty of each day and mark important events in our lives. These rites are just a few of the ways you can use witchcraft to delight in yourself, your friends, and those special once-in-a-lifetime moments. I guarantee that these enchanting rituals will create unforgettable memories and attract glorious blessings into your life.

SONG OF SELF RITUAL FOR SELF-EXPRESSION AND INTROSPECTION

This solo ritual is one that I find particularly entertaining. It requires you to look hard at yourself, but it's also fun. Essential elements that are necessary for this ritual include:

- Big sheets of butcher paper

- Color markers, glitter, beads, shells, cloth, ribbon, yarn—
  whatever colorful materials you respond well to
- Sewing kit and craft boxes with random scraps, buttons, and/or
  shiny objects

It is good to undertake this ritual on a Sunday, but whenever you need support, reserve half an hour of quiet time and brew up some willpower to help you with your self-expression. Light a white candle anointed with peppermint oil and light spicy incense such as cinnamon. Prepare for your Song of Myself by sipping this warm drink for encouragement: Take a sprig of mint (homegrown is best), a cup of warm milk, and cinnamon sticks and stir together clockwise in a white mug. Recite:

> Herb of menthe and spicy mead,
> today is the day I will succeed.
> In every word and every deed.
> Today I sing the song of me.

Drink the brew while it is still warm and "sit for a spell." You will know when you are ready.

Now take the paper and markers and begin your song of yourself. Write with any marker you pick up and finish this sentence at least twenty-four times: *I am* _____. Be as wild and free and true as you can. You are so many things. Express them here and now, once and for all. I will share some wonderful "Songs of Self" that I have seen and heard:

> I am a wild woman.
> I am beautiful.
> I am wide.
> I am a secret.
> I am sexy.
> I am brilliant.
> I am a blue sky.
> I am all possibility.

I am a dream come to life.
I am truth.
I am the Goddess.
I am the living incarnation of wisdom.
I am life.
I am a living blessing.
I am the road.
I am perfect.
I am a tiger.
I am yesterday and today.
I am hope.
I am angry.
I am art.
I am a crone.
I am a sister to the sun.
I am a poem.
I am creative.
I am me!

This can go on as long as you want it to. Only when you feel you have expressed every aspect of yourself should you put down your marker and begin to decorate the paper. Paint on it; glue mirror shards to it; create one or many self-portraits. Scrawl symbols on it. Write more words, allowing yourself total and absolute creative freedom. There is no wrong or right; there is only you and all your myriad aspects. Celebrate yourself and reveal yourself completely. By the end, you should have a one-of-a-kind self-portrait that tells your real story. Hang your self-song portrait in a sacred place, perhaps near your altar or shrine area. Its energy will permeate the place with your personal essence in a wonderful way.

WHISPERS OF HOPES AND DREAMS: A RITUAL TO BLESS YOUR ENGAGEMENT

Engagement is a monumental occasion in a person's life, and so of course it should be celebrated with a little magic to bless your union! The important thing to remember in the engagement process is to make sure you share similar ideas about the path of life. Being engaged is a time to make sure you are compatible on many levels as you enjoy the romance. You will need to have frank discussions on career, home, health, children, sex, and the expectations you have for yourself and your partner in all these areas.

Sometimes when we are in love, we expect people to simply "know" what we want. Magical people expect that even more, feeling that their partner is so intuitive that they should be able to anticipate each other's actions and opinions on these aspects of life. Though it would be ideal, that's not realistic thinking. Sometimes it can be hardest to read those with whom we are closest. A good relationship requires good communication. This formalized engagement ritual involves dream sharing, and therefore, it should only be done after such frank discussions so that nothing comes as a shock. Preparing to perform this ritual is a good way to initiate such talks. It can be done right after the acceptance or at any point later in the engagement process. Just make sure you are both aware of each other's ideas of the future before you begin your life together. When you are ready to move forward and begin the ritual, first go someplace comfortable where you will not be disturbed. This ritual can be done in your home or even at a quiet restaurant or coffee shop. Perhaps you'll want to take your love to the place where you first dated.

Start with your favorite drinks. I like a good wine or champagne, but it doesn't have to be alcoholic, just something you both enjoy and can share. Have three glasses ready. Light three candles: one of your favorite color, one of your betrothed's favorite color, and the third of a color you both like. Unless you choose the same color for all three candles, the third candle should be different from the first two so that neither of you dominates in the energy of the relationship. When in doubt, three white candles work well. Each of you light your candle, and together light the flame of the third with your two candles.

Pour the drink into two of the three glasses, making each about half full. Hold the two glasses near the fire. Don't get too close—you don't want to shatter your glasses. The light, not the heat, is the important part. Speak close to the mouth of the glass, and whisper into the wine your hopes, dreams, and blessings for the marriage. What do you feel? What do you want to do? What do you want to create together? Envisioning a long, healthy, happy life together, you can talk about home, family, and careers. See yourselves supporting each other in separate goals and working together for your joint dreams. You each should speak your words into the liquid. Then pour both drinks into the third empty glass, combining your hopes and dreams. Share that one glass, savoring its flavor and reflecting on your future. Do not speak until you have both finished the combined drink. Look into each other's eyes, and kiss. The ritual is complete.

HANDFASTING RITUAL: A TRADITIONAL PAGAN WEDDING CEREMONY

Weddings are usually planned at least a year ahead. If at all possible, choose a day during the new moon phase, as a marriage is a very important new beginning. Create a bower of beautiful, scented flowers and burn lightly scented candles. Traditional flowers recommended for the bower include roses, cherry and apple blossoms, and gardenias. As a gift at one handfasting, I gave the happy couple long-burning votive candles in a mint-pomegranate scent which lasts for days. On their anniversary, I always give them the same candles so that they can rekindle the moment of their wedding, since smell and memory have powerful ties.

In Western culture, it is customary for the bride to wear a veil and some red and blue in her wedding finery. Giving gifts is also an important part of the convention of weddings. The bride and groom should wrap small, symbolic presents for each other and set them on the altar, which is placed in the eastern part of the room or space. Altar decorations are simple and symbolic: just two white candles and a willow wand. The wedding rings are affixed to the willow wand. At this handfasting, I also gave the bride and groom symbolic gifts of small rings and ribbons of blue to represent the energies of the air, red incense to be lit from the candles to represent the energies of fire, and a gardenia to represent the earth. Wine, which represents water, should be in a chalice on the altar. Wine for all, along with sweet cakes, should also be ready for the celebration and set up to share with the guests and witnesses. Wiccan tradition calls for both a priest and a priestess to perform the handfasting, but in this case, according to the wishes of the bride and groom, I officiated alone.

Since most of this couple's family members were Methodist and Catholic, we wanted to make everyone as comfortable as possible with the concept of a highly ritualistic pagan marriage. We created little cards explaining the origin of the handfasting and provided the text and instructions for audience participation. The cards were tied to little bells to be rung at the end of the ritual to signal through sound that the marriage ceremony had been completed. Not only were the wedding guests comfortable with the ritual, but they also loved it. The bride wore a scarlet wedding dress, a lovely red veil, and a willow wand headdress. The groom wore an elegant tuxedo, which set off her fiery gown perfectly.

Handfasting Ritual

The priest or priestess speaks:

> *May the place of this marriage be consecrated,*
> *for we gather here in the ritual of love and bliss*
> *with two who would be wedded.*
> [Bride's name] *and* [Groom's name]*, please step forward and*
> *stand here before your friends and family and before the gods and*
> *goddesses of the world.*
>
> *Be with us here, O spirits of the air*
> *and with your swift fingers tie the bonds between these two*
> *who would be married, and tie them closely and securely.*
> *Be with us here.*

At this point, tie the two symbolic gift rings together with blue ribbon, then loop them over the willow wand and replace it on the altar.

> *Be with us here, O spirits of fire*
> *and light their love and passion*
> *with your fiery ardor.*

Light the incense from the candles and place it on the altar, then say aloud:

> *Be with us here, O spirits of the earth*
> *and ground deep the roots of their love.*

Pick up the willow wand and tie the gardenia to it. Then say:

Be with us here, O spirits of water
and let joy flow forever for [Groom's name] *and* [Bride's name]*,*
for as long as they are married,
blessed goddess and merry god.
Give to [Groom's name] *and* [Bride's name]*, who stand before us in*
the light of their love, your love and protection.
Blessed be!

Here the audience responds:

Blessed be.

Hold the willow wand with the rings and gardenia tied to it out to the
bride and groom, instructing them:

Place your right hand over this wand and the rings of this rite
of marriage.
Above you are the stars,
below you the stones.
As time passes, think upon this:
like the eastern star, your love shall remain constant.
Like a rock, your love will stand firm.
Possess one another, but always be understanding.
Have patience at all times,
for stormy times come and go, but they leave upon the wind.
Give each other love as often as possible
of the body, the mind, and the spirit.
Be not afraid and do not let the ways of others dissuade you from
your path.
The gods and goddesses are always with you,
now and forever.

After a short pause, ask the bride:

> [Name], *is it your wish to become one with this man?*

She answers.
Ask the groom:

> [Name], *is it your wish to become one with this woman?*

He responds.

> *Does anyone here today say nay?*

Say to the bride and groom:

> *Place the rings on each other now,* [bride] *and* [groom].
> *Before the gods, goddesses, and everyone here as witness,*
> *I now proclaim you husband and wife!*

Now the bride and groom kiss. Next, they speak any words they have prepared for each other. Finally, it's time for them to exchange their symbolic gifts. At the end, say:

> *Now we ring the bells and it is proclaimed—this ritual is done!*

CRONING RITUALS

Our modern society has taken an unfortunate attitude toward aging, characterized by denial and shame. Rather than embracing the realization of their own highest wisdom, aging women are socialized into unhealthy regimens such as Botox and plastic surgery in vain attempts to turn back the clock. Women should feel good about aging; they should celebrate long, full lives. Women should be respected and honored for the wisdom they bring to the community. One of the roles ritual plays in the world is to change the dynamic between a person and her community. Therefore, croning rituals are the signal to the group that a woman has ascended into a new role of service and leadership to the family, the tribe, the village, and the sisterhood. Theories vary as to when a woman becomes a crone. Z. Budapest in her *Holy Book of Women's Mysteries* says it happens to every woman at age fifty-six. Others say it is at age fifty-four, and priestess and writer Diana Paxson says it's a range from sixty to seventy-one for the evolution from Queen to Crone. Often cronehood is confirmed at fourteen months past a woman's last period, and when she has come to her second Saturn Return. A woman should decide for herself when she feels she has reached the age of "cronehood," however; if she is not prepared to take on the title, then by all means she should wait until she is ready. Discussing it with other women will help authenticate what you know and feel inside. Support from the sisterhood is essential, and in many circles of friends and family, women who are of similar ages should sustain each other in life's passages and honor each other as they wish to be honored.

Rite of the Wise Age: A Ceremony to Bestow the Crown of Cronehood

The essential elements for this ritual are enough candles to represent every year of the crone's life, flowers, silver wire, crystals, water, flowering branches, silver moon-shaped paper cutouts, and potluck food. The potluck food served at the party after the ritual will be even more special and good for all if they emphasize "women's food" such as estrogen-filled yams, calcium-rich broccoli, and yogurt. Soy is recommended as well, and chocolate is essential.

The first part of the ritual takes place before the honored guest, the new crone, arrives. Working together, women should take the silver wire and form a round crown. Glue semiprecious crystals to this crown, attach charms and amulets, and affix the silver crescent moons. Make it beautiful and meaningful. The silver moon is a sign of the Goddess, and the new crone is a representative of the Goddess's third aspect. The crystals, which are the stones and bones of Mother Earth, add power and the beauty of Gaia. Charms and amulets are for health, protection, good luck, and good life. As you make it and place the jewels and charms on the crown, state your intentions and hopes for the new crone. When the crown is complete, place it on a beautiful purple pillow or on the altar.

Upon the arrival of the soon-to-be-crowned crone, the eldest woman present should take a flowering branch and dip it in water and sprinkle it on her head, just a few drops, and speak a blessing, such as:

> *I bless you in the name of the Goddess.*
> *I bless you in the name of Mother Earth.*
> *I bless you in the name of every woman.*
> *Sister, do you accept the role of teacher and leader as crone?*

The crone responds. If she accepts the title, then the eldest woman says:

> *She is crowned.*

Now the elder places the Crown of Cronehood upon the new crone's head. Go around the circle and have each woman speak of the gift she added to the crown; here are examples:

> *I give you amethyst to represent the healing power of the planet.*
> *I give you silver, sacred to the moon.*
> *I give you roses, the flower of desire.*
> *I give you a sacred heart charm to represent the mysteries of love.*
> *I give you a blue star because you are a star.*
> *I give you an abalone shell because you are powerful like the ocean.*
> *I give you moonstone because you are wise and reflective.*

I give you an angel pendant because you are so beautiful in body and in soul.

Now everyone should speak together:

We gather together to celebrate that [new crone's name] *is entering the Wise Age.*

Now the eldest woman lights one candle, and then each woman present in turn lights a candle until all fifty-six (or the appropriate number equaling this crone's age) candles are lit.

Singing and chanting now take place with the circle holding hands:

[Crone's name]*, Lady Mine,*
We now honor you; we will never forsake you.
[Crone's name]*, we listen to your wisdom with the love of our hearts.*
We accept your teachings with ears and hands.
Blessed be the new crone! Long life and good health! Happiness and joy!

After everyone has spoken her tribute to the crone, she can speak her thanks. At this point, the crone assumes her leadership role. Leadership is best handled with great gravity and lightness at the same time. "Benevolence" and "wisdom" are the watchwords. The crone should speak anything she is holding in her heart. Doubtless, she will want to speak her gratitude for the support of the sisterhood, but she should also speak forth any concerns she has. The concerns can be specific to her world, which is now her domain—her family, her group of friends, her spiritual circle, her community, or even the planet. The crone can choose to ask a pair of disputing friends to make up and work it out. She can request that a healing garden be made for her people. Whatever comes to her mind that will be helpful and essential to the group and the greater good is what she should speak. I know a crone who has asked people to help her build a community center, and it is happening.

I know another crone who quit her high-powered corporate job to study the medicine wheel and become a shaman. Still another elder has taken up the brush and is painting beautiful art after years of working for the defense department; this is my mother, Helen, who is a wonderful example of the power of cronehood. When the crone has spoken from the wisdom of her heart, everyone should again hold hands. The eldest woman who inducted the new crone again holds out the flowering branch and hands it to the new crone. The crone speaks her blessing to everyone present, touching everyone's heads with a few drops of blessing water and saying words from her heart to each person. When she is done, she says: *This circle is now open. Blessed be to all.*

Now the food is served, and it should be a birthday party to remember for the rest of the crone's life.

REVEALING THE TRUE SELF: A GROUP MASK-MAKING RITUAL

The elements needed for this ritual include:

- Posterboard, newspaper, water, and white flour to make a plaster-like paste, paint, glitter, feathers, sequins, colored markers, and sticks at least twelve inches long

- Music—harem music, women's opera choruses, Eastern European women's choral singing

- Butcher paper (also tape large pieces of butcher paper to the wall)

- Scarves

Whatever room you're in, create a sacred space there. Light incense, lamps, and candles, and put on belly dancing or other women's music.

Lay out the mask-making supplies on tables covered with butcher paper. Build a little cardboard wall between mask-making stations to create privacy so each participant feels completely comfortable in disclosing a heretofore hidden side of her sacred self. Before starting to make her mask, each woman in turn should step up to a piece of paper on the wall and state aloud the positive qualities she sees in herself. She should proclaim her affirming, esteem-boosting aspects. This should be as free-form and upbeat as possible.

After the personal statements, other women should chime in with encouraging words. It is amazing to hear the unexpected perceptions of others, and this part of the experience can be life changing. Write everything down. Each woman should then take her affirmations to her workstation. These words will be the source of inspiration for masks of power and beauty.

Next, draw a large version of the mask you envision and cut it out, making sure you have holes for your eyes, nose, and mouth. Mix the white flour and water into a thin glue. Take your newspaper, tear it into strips, and glue it onto your mask shape. Remember to create the features for your mask face, such as a long nose or a beak; use your imagination to the fullest. After it has dried a bit, you can begin shaping the mask into a curve to fit over your face, and then glue on the decorations and adornments. Now, turn up the women's music, and with paint, glue, and glitter, create an expression of your inner and outer beauty on paper. Listen to the throbbing drums and the hypnotic beats; listen to your own inner rhythms.

Eventually, each woman will finish one or more masks. Glue a stick to the side or base of each mask so that they can be held over the face like Venetian masquerade masks. As these masks dry, dance to the music. When everyone's masks are dry, each woman should reveal her "secret" self. She can take a turn and step out into the middle of the room, wearing a veil or scarf over her mask. Before casting off the protective veil, each woman should announce her revelatory self. An example might be: "I am the Fire Goddess" or "I am the Selkie of the Irish Coast." I did a self-portrait mask of "Peacock Girl" that profoundly affected my life. Every time I see it, I feel reaffirmed.

All of the beautiful, masked women should dance together to the music and raise the energy in the room. While this is taking place, the level of self-esteem in the room will skyrocket.

Our masks should be kept as totems to be worn in the event of poor self-image. Hang your mask on the wall in your bedroom or office as a constant reminder of your true and beautiful self.

SATURN-DAY SOUL TRIBE GATHERING

It is very important to gather your soul tribe and just celebrate each other from time to time. Here is a pagan ritual I have performed on weekends—I call it "Saturn-day night fever." Over the years, I have added many embellishments, such as astrological or holiday themes. The basic ritual of cakes and ale, however, is a timeless and powerful classic.

Gather a group of friends either outdoors under the moon or in a room large enough for dancing, drumming, and singing. Have the guests bring a cake of their choice as well as a cider, mead, beer, or juice to share. (Note that the cake can be of any style, so it does not have to be an iced sheet cake; banana bread, Irish soda bread, or a braided honey bread will do just as well.) Place the offerings in the center, on an altar table. Then light green and brown candles for home and hearth.

Once everyone is seated, the host or designated leader intones:

> *Gods of Nature, bless these cakes,*
> *that we may never suffer hunger.*
> *Goddess of the Harvest, bless this ale,*
> *that we may never go without drink.*

The eldest and the youngest of the circle rise and serve the food and drink to everyone in the circle. Last, they serve each other. The ritual leader pronounces the blessing again. Then everyone says together, "Blessed be."

The feasting begins, ideally followed by a lot more ale and lively dancing. A wonderful way to keep a group of friends connected is for a different person to host the circle one Saturday each month.

11

RITUALS FOR THE SEASONS AND HOLIDAYS

In my opinion, there is no better way to celebrate the holidays than with a festive ritual. The seasonal rites and revels you will find in this chapter hearken back to time-honored pagan traditions that have been observed for thousands of years. When I partake in them, I like to think about our predecessors and the ways these practices make me feel connected to them, as well as the rich histories and cultures that influence and inform the way that we modern witches practice witchcraft in the twenty-first century. These rituals celebrate the cycles of life and death and the changing of the seasons, honor the gods and goddesses, pay respect to our ancestors, and more, ensuring that we always have a reminder to practice gratitude and rejoice in the bounties and blessings we have received in our lives. But remember, Dear Reader, that you don't need to wait for a holiday to celebrate. Each new day lived on this majestic earth is cause for its own celebration!

GATHER ROUND THE FIRE: A COMMUNITY NEEDFIRE RITUAL FOR WINTER

Without fire, there would be no life. For this ritual, gather together members of your community to participate in honoring the life-giving power of flame.

Supplies:

- Altar space
- Wood, matches, kindling, and a safe place for a fire
- Candles
- Cauldron or large pot
- Ice cubes, water
- Drums
- Fire tool or poker
- Apples, apple cider, or apple ice cream
- White ice cream
- Spoons and bowls
- Bowl with tarot cards in it

1. Place the bowl of tarot cards on the space designated as the altar.

2. Ask for a volunteer to be in charge of the fire and to be the leader of the ritual. The fire maker should then select three women to represent the Norns (a.k.a. the Three Fates). One of the fates will be in charge of "giving fire." With a candle in the cauldron, she keeps the fire safe and gives it to the fire maker. Another fate reads out the future to ritual participants with a one-card tarot reading. The last fate gives life in the form of the ritual foods—the apples, hot cider, ice cream, and so on.

3. The participants should get as cold as possible before beginning the ritual—take off your coats and sweaters, and open all the windows and doors if you are inside. You need to feel the winter deep in your soul. The leader should pass around the ice cubes so the participants engage in a sensory way with freezing cold and the need for fire.

4. While the participants get good and chilly, the leader should start the fire. People who really want the totally authentic experience of firemaking can try to create fire from sparking with a fire drill, but the ritual could then take hours unless the fire maker is well practiced in the art of making fire.

5. The following is the chant to be spoken while the fire is being made. The ritual leader should pass out the drums and begin leading rhythmic sounds to underscore the chanting.

> *Winter winds howl and wail.*
> *We feel the cold in our bones.*
> *This is an old familiar tale.*
> *The ice binds and surrounds us all.*
> *Fates above, please hear our call.*
> *Fire thaws the ice.*
> *Fire creates the water.*
> *The heat warms our bones.*
> *Fire and ice bind our lives.*
> *Now feel the fire!*

6. Holding hands, everyone should dance slowly around the fire sunwise, feeling the life-giving warmth. Next, repeat the chant.

7. The fate of the future goes around the circle with the bowl of tarot cards and performs one-card readings for each individual. If time

allows, she should also do a reading for the group with the full set of tarot cards about the future of the community.

8. Last, the fate who gives life serves the group celebratory food— the ice cream and other cold foods are a remembrance of the cold of the icy times, and the hot cider and other hot foods represent the life-giving heat of fire. The head of the ritual should lead everyone in a discussion of the importance of the ritual of the needfire and any other topic important to every participant and the community.

FEBRUARY 2ND RITUAL FOR CANDLEMAS

Candlemas, the highest point of spiritual power between the winter solstice and the spring equinox, is also known as Imbolc, Brigid's Day, and the Feast of the Purification of the Virgin. Many Wiccans use this sabbat (holy day) as the special day to initiate new witches. Brigid, the Celtic goddess and saint honored on this day, is connected with both the elements of fire and water, both powerful powers of purification.

Essential elements for this Candlemas ritual are a cauldron, white candles, a bough of cedar, a small bough of pine, a small bough of juniper, a small bough of holly, incense, red cotton thread or yarn, a stone for an altar, and a bowl of water.

The leader of the circle should purify the circle with the fire of the incense while invoking the four directions to raise power. Place your altar stone north of the circle, and place white candles on and around the altar. Cast the circle:

Face east and say:

Welcome, Guardians of the East, bringing your fresh winds, the breath of life.
Come to the Circle on Candlemas.

Face south and say:

> *Welcome, Guardians of the South, bringing us heat and health.*
> *Come to the circle on Candlemas.*

Face west and say:

> *Welcome, Guardians of the West, bringing the setting sun and*
> *nourishing gentle rains.*
> *Come to the circle on Candlemas.*

Face north and say:

> *Welcome, Guardians of the North, bringing life-bringing rains and*
> *snow.*
> *Come to the circle on Candlemas.*

While meditating on the concept of purification, make a bouquet of
the four branches and wrap it near the bottom with the red cord. The
red symbolizes Brigid's fiery aspect, while the four trees stand for
purification. Bow with it to each of the four directions. Bow last to the
north, over the altar stone, and say:

> *Bright Brigid,*
> *Sweep clean our homes and spirits on this sacred day.*
> *Purify our souls of the dullness of winter, and help us prepare for*
> *the light of summer.*
> *Brigid of the white hands, Brigid of the golden curls,*
> *Bless us all. So mote it be.*

All respond:

> *So mote it be!*

The ritual leader dips the tips of the branches in the water and sprinkles the circle and each participant, saying:

Blessed Brigid, may your water heal us and make us whole.

Leave the bouquet on the altar stone as an offering to Brigid.

THE SPRING EQUINOX: RITUAL FOR OSTARA

At this time, celebrate the festival of Ostara (a.k.a. Eoster), the Saxon goddess who is the personification of the rising sun. Her totem is the rabbit. Legend has it that her rabbit brought forth the brightly colored eggs now associated with Easter. At this time the world is warming under the sun as spring approaches. Every plant, animal, man, and woman feels this growing fever for spring.

This ritual is intended for communities, so gather a group. Tell everyone to bring a "spring food" such as deviled eggs, salads with flowers in them, freshly made broths, berries, mushrooms, fruits, pies, veggie casseroles, and quiches. Have the food table at the opposite side of the area away from the altar, but decorate it with flowers and pussy willow branches that are just beginning to bud, the harbingers of spring.

Essential elements for this ritual are an altar table; a cot; bay laurel leaves; bowls of water; multicolored crystals; candles; a jar of honey; fruits of colors including yellow, red, white, and purple; musical instruments; and one bowl each of seeds, leaves, flowers, and fruit.

Create your own Ostara altar in the middle of the ritual area by covering the table with a cloth in a color that represents spring to you. It could be a richly hued flowered cloth or a light green one in a solid color. The cloth should represent new life. Scatter bay laurel leaves around the table. Place goddesses on the altar table, too, with Ostara at the center. Put colored eggs, chocolate rabbits, candles, and crystals around the goddesses. In the east, set a yellow candle and crystals of amber, gold, and yellow such as citrine or agate. Place yellow fruit such as pears or bananas in front of the candle as an offering to the energies of the east. In the south, set a red candle and red and orange stones such as garnet or the newly available "rough rubies," which cost only a few cents each. Apples and pomegranates are excellent red foods to place in front of this candle. In the west, set a purple candle with amethysts in front of it. Sweet plums are a perfect fruit to place in front of the candle, perhaps with some purple berries. In the north, set a white candle and a clear quartz or white crystal. Honeydew melon is an appropriate selection for the fruit offering.

Choose four representatives to invoke the directions.

East—Everyone faces east. The representative for the direction should weave a story and create a vision that can be shared by all that evokes new beginnings, such as the rising of the morning sun. Spring is the time for renewal and growth in nature. The speaker can, for example, take the bowl of seeds and tell the tale of the seeds sprouting in the dark moist soil of Mother Earth. Pass the bowl of seeds around to everyone, and urge them to take some seeds home to plant.

South—Everyone faces south. The speaker for this direction should invoke the power of the leaf. Leaves draw in the energy of the sun through photosynthesis and help keep an important cycle of life moving. Leaves grow throughout the summer season, drinking in the water of life and using the power of the sun for photosynthesis. Pass the bowl of leaves around to everyone in the group.

West—Everyone faces west. The speaker for this direction should invoke the power of flowers. Flowers bud and bloom. They follow the sun and are some of nature's purest expressions of beauty. Flowers bring joy to people, and many flowers become fruit. Pass the bowl of flowers to the group and urge everyone to take some.

North—Everyone faces the north. The speaker for the north should invoke fruit and harvest time. Fruit is the result of nature's generosity. Fruit also contains the seeds for our future. Pass the bowl of fruit around and suggest everyone take one and eat it, meditating on the glory and deep meaning it contains. If it is appropriate, you can also offer juice or wine as part of the fruit invocation. Wine is the glorious nectar of fruit.

Now it's time for the ritual enactment. Everyone takes a seat around the altar. Drummers should start to play a gentle rhythm. Chanting, singing, and ululating are also encouraged, however people feel comfortable expressing themselves.

Each speaker should in turn light a candle and invoke the ancestors of the group. Remembrances to people who have died in the past year are an important respect that may be paid to the community at large.

Next is the honoring of the moon. Ask people to speak about the moon, reciting their favorite moon poems or moon memories.

Anointing the third eye blesses your insight for the coming year. Pass the bowls of water and laurel leaves around. Take a leaf and dip it in the water, then touch the wet leaf to your third eye. Pass the bowl on to the next person. When the bowl has made its way back to the ritual leader, sing and dance in celebration of spring.

Everyone should get in a line and hold hands and dance around the circle like a plant moving and growing, flowering and fruiting. When the four speakers feel that the energy has reached a climax, each one should clap and say in turn:

And now it is done; now it is spring!

They open the circle by saying together:

It is spring in the East, it is spring in the South, it is spring in the West, and it is spring in the North!

REVELING IN LOVE AND LUST: A BELTANE TRYST

Beltane is the sexiest high holiday for witches and one that is anticipated all year. I always look forward to having a joyful "spree" every May. Witches begin to celebrate Beltane on the last night of April, and it is traditional for the festivities to last all night. This is a time for feasting, dancing, laughter, and lots of lovemaking. The Celts of old made this day a day of wild abandon, a sexual spree, the one day of the year when it is okay to make love outside your relationship. On May Day, when the sun returns in the morning, revelers gather to erect a merrily beribboned Maypole to dance around, followed by picnicking and sensual siestas.

Ideally, celebrate outdoors, but if you are stuck indoors on Beltane Eve, pick a place with a fireplace and have a roaring blaze so celebrants can wear comfy clothing and dance barefoot. Ask them to bring spring flowers and musical instruments, including plenty of drums! Place pillows on the floor and serve a sensual feast of foods from the following list, under the title "Oral Fixations," along with beer, wine, ciders, and honeyed mead that you can make or obtain from a microbrewery. Gather some of spring's bounty of flowers—roses, tulips, and my favorite, freesias, in your favorite colors, or whatever is blooming with the most vitality where you live. Set out candles in spring colors—yellow, pink, red, green, white, purple. With your arms extended, point to each of the four directions and say, "To the east, to the south, to the west, and to the north," and recite this Beltane rhyme:

> *Hoof and horn, hoof and horn,*
> *tonight our spirits are reborn.* [repeat thrice]
> *Welcome joy into my home,*
> *fill my friends with love and laughter.*
> *So mote it be.*

Have each guest light a candle and speak to the subject of love with a toast of Beltane Brew. Drumming and dancing is the next part of the circle. This is truly an invocation of lust for life and will be a night to remember for all. Now rejoice!

Oral Fixations

Food can be foreplay, a wonderful prelude to a night of love. I recommend consuming these aphrodisiacs for your pleasure:

- **Almonds**, or erotically shaped marzipan
- **Arugula**, also called "rocket"
- **Avocado**, referred to by the ancient Aztecs as the "testicle tree"
- **Bananas** and **banana flowers**
- **Chocolate**, quite rightly called "the food of the gods"
- **Honey**, as the term "honeymoon" came from a bee-sweetened drink served to newlyweds
- **Nutmeg**, the traditional aphrodisiac for Chinese women; eat enough and you will hallucinate
- **Oysters**, prized by the Romans for both their effect and their resemblance to female genitalia
- **Strawberries**, often mentioned in erotic literature
- **Coffee**, a stimulant for many things
- **Garlic**, the heat to light the flame of desire
- **Figs**, another symbol of ultimate femininity; just eating one is a turn-on
- **Vanilla**, captivating for both its scent and its flavor

MIDSUMMER DAY:
A SUMMER SOLSTICE RITE

Essential elements for a Celtic-inspired Midsummer ritual are a wooden wheel, fallen branches and firewood, multicolored candles (and also torches, if you can acquire them), multicolored ribbons, food and drink, and flowers for garlands. This ritual should be performed outside, ideally on a hill or mountaintop at dusk. Call the local fire department to verify the fire laws in your area. You will likely need a special permit to light a bonfire, and certain areas may be restricted. Always clear the grass and brush away from your fire area, and make sure to dig a shallow pit into the ground. Circle the pit with rocks to help mark the edge of the fire pit as well as to contain the accidental spread of fire. Have a fire extinguisher, a pail of sand, and water bottles nearby in case the fire gets out of control. One person not directly involved in the ritual who is designated as the fire-tender should be on hand to watch the fire at all times; be sure to find a constant and observant volunteer for this quiet yet vital duty. Make sure the fire pit is far enough away from surrounding trees and other landscape features to allow room for a group to dance around it.

Lay the wooden wheel down in the circle of stones, and arrange the fallen branches and firewood around the edge of it. The wheel represents the turning of the year, and the sun on its daily and yearly cycle. Tie the colored ribbons on the nearest tree. While these preparations are being made, the priestess to lead the ritual should meditate in the area where the ritual will be held, focusing on connecting to the goddess. The gathered celebrants should weave garlands of flowers while the sun slowly sets. Just before the sun vanishes completely, the priestess should direct participants to ready their candles, or even better, torches. The priest lights them, declaring:

> *The fire festival is begun.*
> *Under this longest day of the sun.*
> *Let us go forth and make merry.*
> *The god and goddess are here!*

All say:

Blessed be!

The priest leads the celebrants into the circle where the priestess waits and directs them to throw their torches and candles in the bonfire. The priestess raises her arms and invokes the Goddess:

Great Earth Mother and Lady of the Forest,
be with us here and now!
On this night the Goddess reigns supreme.
On this, our Midsummer's night!

All say:

Blessed be!

All should dance in the direction of the sun (clockwise) around the fire, raise their arms, and clap and shout for joy for as long as they want. When people begin to tire, it is time for the feast. The priest directs the blessing of the food:

Blessed Lady of the Forest,
Old gods of the animals, spirits of the wild,
bless this food and drink,
that it may strengthen us in your ways.

All say:

Blessed be!

Everyone should share in the refreshments and eat, drink, and make merry. Another round of dance and song is in order. When the bonfire has turned to ash, the priestess declares the ritual to be over and says:

Our revelry this day is done, dear one.
Gods of the old and spirits of nature,
we thank you for your blessings this night.
This rite is done.

All say:

Blessed be!

Make certain the fire has completely gone out before you leave the ritual site. Soak the ashes with water and clean up the site. Always leave a natural area cleaner than you found it.

LAMMAS DAY: A RITUAL OF GRATITUDE FOR THE CHANGING OF SEASONS

Essential elements for this ritual are sheaves of grain (such as wheat or barley), a cauldron, water, one floating candle, one candle for each person present, and essential oils of rose, lavender, or other summer flowers.

Your Lammas Day ritual should be held on August first, the beginning of the harvest season in the ancient cycle of the year. To create the sacred space of the ritual, arrange the sheaves of grain in the four directions around a cauldron. Fill the cauldron three-quarters full with water, then add essential oils of the flowers of summer. Cast your circle in the usual manner.

At this point, the leader of the ritual should light the candles and then hand them to each person and guide the participants to form a circle around the cauldron. Now the floating candle should be lit and placed in the cauldron by the leader, who says:

> *O Ancient Lugh of days long past,*
> *be here with us now*
> *in this place between worlds,*
> *on this Lammas Day.*

Rap three times on the cauldron and say:

> *Harvest is here and the seasons do change,*
> *this is the height of the year.*
> *The bounty of summer sustains us*
> *in spirit, in soul, and in body.*

Now the group circles five times around the cauldron. All present should then speak their gratitude for the gifts of the season and the riches of the summer's bounty. Storytelling, singing, and dancing should all be a part of this rite; when the tales have been told and the songs have been sung, the leader determines when the rite is done by putting out the candles and proclaiming:

> *This rite is done!*

Close the circle.

You can create your own variations on this Lammas Day celebration, incorporating your own views on the summer season and how you show appreciation to nature and spirit. One lovely way to celebrate Lammas Day, anciently named *Lughnasa* in Celtic cultures, is to have a feast that begins and ends with gratitude and blessings for the food and wine, with a place set and food set aside for the great godly guest, Lugh.

SACRED ALTAR OF AUTUMN: A FALL EQUINOX RITUAL

Establish one room in your house as the temple. Ideally, it is the room in which you normally keep an altar or sacred shrine. In any case, you should create an altar in the center of the space. Place four small tables in the four directions, which may be closest to either the walls or the room's corners, and place four evenly spaced candlesticks between the tables. Place a loaf of freshly baked bread (bread you have made with your own hands is best) in the east, a bowl of apples in the south, a bottle of wine in the west, and a sheaf of wheat or a bundle of dried corn in the north.

Upon the main altar, place a candle, a plate of sweet cakes, and a goblet. Light incense and place it in front of the cakes. Before your ritual, take some time for contemplation. Think about what you have achieved during this busy year:

- What have you done?
- What do you need?
- What remains to be done?
- What are your aspirations?

Write down your thoughts and feelings and the answers to those questions. Read what you have written and ponder it. Look for continuing ideas or themes, and make notes of these on a piece of paper. Next, take a calming and cleansing quiet bath, and snip a lock of your freshly washed hair and place it on the paper where you wrote your notes. Dress yourself in a robe that feels right for making magic and enter your temple space. Light the candle on the altar, and use this candle to light all the other candles in the temple. Speak the traditional Hebrew words of self-blessing:

Ateh, Malkuth, Ve Geburah, Ve Gedulah, Le Olahm, Amen:
through the symbol of the pentagram in the name of Adonai.

Repeat this facing each corner, and then face your altar and say:

> *In the east, Raphael; in the south, Michael; in the west, Gabriel;*
> *in the north, Uriel.*
> *Welcome to this place in the name of Melchisedec, the High Priest*
> *of the Godhead.*

Then go to the east, and raising the loaf of bread in a gesture of offering, say:

> *Raphael, Lord of the Winds of Heaven, bless this bounty born of sun*
> *and air and earth.*
> *Let us feed the hungry and bless the hand that gives it.*

Place the bread back into the bowl and go to the southern corner. Raise an apple in offering and state:

> *Michael, protector of the weak and the oppressed, bless this sun-*
> *ripened fruit,*
> *and let it be not the fruit of temptation but the fruit of our*
> *knowledge,*
> *so we know how to make our choices and understand the measure*
> *of both good and evil.*

Place the apple back into the bowl and go to the western corner. Lifting up the bottle of wine, say:

> *Gabriel, bringer of the word of God, bless this wine that we may*
> *take into our body*
> *the wine of life shed by all saviors since time began.*

Place the bottle back on the western table. Turn to the north, and raising the corn or wheat as an offering, say:

Uriel, Lord of the Earth and all its bounty, bless this crop
that it may be plentiful all over the earth,
that this may be a year when all humankind
will know the comfort of food and hearth.

Now return to the altar in the center of the temple. Light the incense and place some bread and the chalice of wine on the altar. Dip a piece of bread into the blessing wine. Proclaim:

Melchisedec, priest of the most high God, in the desert after the battle
with the kings of Edom you brought bread and wine to Abraham. In
this communion shared between man and priest of the most high God,
a covenant was made. I pray that this coming harvest makes bread
for the world. In token of the ancient custom, I take this bread and
wine into my body. Now in this sacred place, guide and teach me,
show me how to pursue knowledge for the power of good. Help me to
grow in wisdom. Bless me. Bless those who share my life. Bless all of
those with whom I work. Bless this earth, this sweet, green world that
gives us all the blessings we enjoy—all the water and wine, all the corn
and wheat, all the joys of life in this body. Bless my home.

Take a lock of hair, light it from the candle, and burn it in the bowl of incense, saying:

This is the offering of myself.
In the east—blessings to Raphael.
In the south—blessings to Michael.
In the west—blessings to Gabriel.
In the north—blessings to Uriel.
Blessed be to all.

Now go around your temple space in reverse order, extinguishing all candles. Then declare your temple closed. The common wisdom is that you should place the apples, bread, and wine in your garden the next day as an offering and a blessing to all of nature.

DIWALI RITUAL TO RELEASE OLD RESENTMENTS AND WELCOME IN THE NEW LIGHT OF HOPE

Diwali offers us the opportunity to vanquish our own demons and start anew. The symbols of light and sweetness are used here to represent the intention to replace resentment and bitterness with hope and the balm of healing and positive energy. Essential elements of this ritual are plenty of candles, a new piece of clothing (such as a scarf) or a new item of jewelry, and a plate of sweet cakes, confections, or candy.

Light as many candles as you can in the room where you are performing this ritual. Create a circle of candles, and create sacred space by having a symbol of each element in your circle: a dish of salt or earth, a cup of water, incense, and a candle. Sit lotus-style in the center of your circle and relax in the flickering candlelight, feeling the center of your circle. Feel the presence of the four elements and the balance they create. Notice how warm and alive the room feels. Notice how the gentle, flickering candlelight makes you feel safe. Now think back to all the difficult situations you have experienced over the past year, including the people who have angered or hurt you. Imagine them surrounded by the warm, loving candlelight, and say to each of them, one by one:

I release you. May the lights of Diwali bless you.

As you release each person or situation, visualize their image melting into the candlelight. While the image fades from your mind's eye, place a bite of the cake or confection in tour mouth. Allow the treat to dissolve, spreading its sweetness across your tongue. Visualize and feel that sweetness spreading through you, counteracting any of the traces of pain or bitterness that might remain. This is the sweetness that your new life holds, untainted by these bitter demons that have held you back. When you have finished releasing your demons to the light, purify the new piece of clothing or item of jewelry by passing it through the smoke of the incense. Put on your new piece of jewelry of clothing, saying:

> *With this act, I declare the past gone, and I see the future bright with hope.*

Stay within your circle of light as long as you desire. Leave some of the cake or sweets as an offering to the gods in thanks for your new life.

PAGAN NEW YEAR: A SOLO RITUAL FOR SAMHAIN

Samhain, also known as the Celtic New Year, is the most profound, important, and best known of all pagan sabbats. Samhain is perhaps the favorite Celtic high holiday of all. After all, it is the witches' New Year celebration and the time to honor and commune with your elders and family members who have passed on to the other side, as well as the time to celebrate the passing year and set intentions for new blessings in the new year to come.

Supplies:

- Altar space
- 8 candles
- Powdered incense
- Bread
- Salt
- Wine

1. Prepare for this most holy night and rite by setting up an altar. Place three candles on a stone altar to represent the Triple Goddess and five to represent the points of the pentagram. The star of the pentagram should be drawn with powdered incense of the self-lighting variety to be lit later. Gather together bread, salt, and wine for the sacrament.

2. After you have made your preparations for the altar, ready yourself by bathing and meditating. Anoint your body before dressing in a robe or gown befitting this night when the veil between the worlds is the thinnest. As you ready your body, mind, and spirit, consider what has taken place in the preceding year. Cleanse your mind and heart of old sorrows and most especially of angers and petty resentments. Bring only your best into this night. After all, this is New Year's Eve for witches, and you want to truly connect with those who have gone on to the other side.

3. Walk alone to the place of the ceremony and kneel before the altar. Before lighting the candles on the altar, say aloud:

   This candle I light for the Maiden's brightest glory.

   Light the candle and bow to the Maiden.

   This candle I light for the power and passion of the Lady, the Queen.

   Light the candle and bow to the Queen.

   This candle I light for the unsurpassable wisdom of the Crone.

   Light the candle and bow to the Crone.

4. Light the incense, and then gazing at the candles on the altar, say:

These do I light in honor of the Triple Goddess
on this sacred night of Samhain.
I create this holy temple
in honor of the Goddess and the God
and all the ancient ones.
From time before time,
I pay my tribute and my devotion
In love and greeting to those beyond the veil.

5. Now light the candles that represent the power of the five-pointed pentagram. Rap three times on the altar with your hands or with your wand. Then say:

   This is a time outside of time
   in a place outside of any place
   on a day that is not a day
   between the worlds and afar.

6. Pause and listen to your heart for thirteen beats, then hold your hands in benediction over the bread, salt, and wine. Now say:

   For this bread, salt, and wine,
   I do ask the blessings
   of our Maiden, our Queen, and our Crone
   and of the God who guards the Gates of the World.

7. Take the bread and sprinkle a bit of salt over it, saying:

   I ask that I and all whom I love
   have health and abundance and blessings.

   Eat the bread, and hold up the goblet of wine, saying:

To a spirit that remains strong and true!

Drink the wine and declare:

By the Triple Goddess and her godly consort, so mote it be!

8. At this point, a danse macabre to any dark folk or Gothic music of your choosing can end the ritual—I suggest any music by the band Dead Can Dance. You should also spend time meditating or allowing yourself to ease into a trance state to communicate with your beloved dead. Hear the messages they have for you and let them know you.

9. When you feel the ritual has ended, quench the candles, and then say:

> *Though these flames*
> *of the material world*
> *be darkened,*
> *they shall ever burn*
> *in the world beyond.*
> *This rite is ended.*

THE SUN RETURNS: A WINTER SOLSTICE RITUAL

Winter solstice rituals traditionally celebrate the rebirth of the sun. In a safe place outdoors, build a bonfire and create a solstice altar to the east of it. Place a small cauldron with a candle in it on the altar, and surround it with mistletoe, ivy, and holly. Participants should also wear crowns woven from these evergreens. If it is too cold or snowy where you live, you can gather indoors and form a semicircle either around the fireplace or around the altar.

Begin the ritual by holding hands around the fire. Hum softly, gradually building the hum to a shout. This shout represents the cries of the Goddess giving birth once again to the sun, and to the new year. The ritual leader says:

> *All bow to the East! Hail to the newborn Sun, and to the Great Goddess who has brought him forth!*

Everyone bows to honor the Sun God and the Mother Goddess. The ritual leader chants:

> *Brigid,*
> *Diana,*
> *Morgan,*
> *Cerridwen,*
> *Heaven's Queen,*
> *by the light of this moon*
> *in this dark night,*
> *teach us the mystery of rebirth.*

The ritual leader lights the candle in the cauldron while everyone else remains perfectly still. Now is the time when the Goddess will reveal herself privately to each participant. If you are outdoors, listen and look carefully for a sign. Traditional omens are a sudden wind, shooting stars, the screeching of an owl, or the appearance of a deer. Even if you are indoors by the fire, the Goddess will still make herself known in your heart. When the time feels right, the ritual leader says:

> *Queen of the Stars,*
> *Queen of the Moon,*
> *Queen of the Earth,*
> *Bringer of Fire,*
> *the Great Mother gives birth to this new year*
> *and we are her witnesses.*

Everyone shouts:

Blessed be!

Pass the lit cauldron to each participant so they can speak a blessing for the new year and the newly reborn sun. Place the cauldron with the candle back on the altar. The ritual leader closes the ritual with this final expression of gratitude to the Goddess:

Blessed be to the Mother Goddess.
Thank you for the sun that gives us life
without beginning and without end
everlasting in eternity.
this ritual is now done!

A toast to the new sun should take place with hot cider or mead and warm festive foods.

THE LONGEST NIGHT OF WINTER: FIRE CEREMONY FOR YULE

December is named for the Roman goddess Decima, one of the three fates. The word Yule comes from the Germanic *jol*, which means midwinter, which is celebrated on the shortest day of the year. The old tradition was to have a vigil all night at a bonfire to make sure the sun did indeed rise again. This primeval custom evolved to become a storytelling evening, and while it may well to be too cold to sit outside in snow and sleet, it is important for your community to congregate around a blazing hearth fire, feasting and talking deep into the night, to truly know each other, impart wisdom, and speak to hopes and dreams. Greet the new sun with stronger connections and a shared vision for the coming solar year.

What you need:

- Candles in the following colors: red, yellow, green, blue, white, and black
- Herbs: tobacco, rosemary, lavender, cedar, sage, and rose petals
- Incense: copal, myrrh, frankincense, or any resin-based incense
- 2 cups sugar
- 1 chocolate bar per person
- Bells, rattles, drums, and other noisemakers
- A firepot, fireplace, or other safe place for an outdoor fire
- Paper for written intentions

The candle colors represent the six directions: north, south, east, west, up, and down (or sky and earth). They also represent the different peoples of the world.

Gather your friends together at dusk on the shortest day of the year and ask them to bring a colored candle (assign each of them a color), a noisemaker, and an open mind. Ask them also to write out what they want to purge from their life and bring the paper into the circle. The Solstice Fire Ceremony serves to bring positive new influences into our lives and to dispel what no longer serves for good. This "letting go" can be anything. For me, one year ago, it was cancer, and this year, it was too much clutter. For you, it could be an unhealthy relationship, a job that makes you miserable, or a cramped apartment.

Yule Ritual

Build a fire at five o'clock in the evening and have it burning brightly as your guests arrive. Place a big bowl of herbs, flower petals, and incense near the fire.

Create a circle around the fire and ask the eldest in the group to slowly draw a circle of sugar around the fire.

When the elder has moved back into place in the circle, each person should light his or her candles from the fire and place it in the sugar circle, creating a mandala.

Ask the youngest person to lead the group in this chant:

My life is my own I must but choose to be better,
vital breath of life I breathe
no more pain and strife!
Wise ones, bring us health and life
bring us love and luck
bring us blessed peace
on this Winter's Day.
Into the fire, we toss the old,
into the fire, we see our future
on this, our longest night.
Harm to none and health to all!

Everyone should rattle and drum away, making merry and rousing the good spirits. The spirits of the wise elders will join you.

After the drumming, start around the circle, beginning with the eldest. Allow people to speak about what they want to release from their life, and have them toss their "letting go" paper into the fire. Then the eldest person should lead the group in a prayer for collective hopes for the coming your, and anyone who wants to add something should also speak out wishes for positive change, for themselves and for the world.

Thank the wise elders and ancestors for their wisdom and spiritual aid by throwing some chocolate into the fire. Be sure to keep some for members of the circle to share and enjoy. The Mayans held the belief that a plentitude of offerings to the ancestors would bring more blessings. They also believed that fire ceremonies helped support the planet and all the nations of the word. Gifts to the fire signal to the elders that they can return through the door and to the other world, until you call upon them for help in the future.

12

WITCH CRAFTS:
DIY CANDLES, ELIXIRS, AND INCENSE

If you are at all crafty like myself, you may find great joy in these DIY witch crafts! Let your creativity shine while enhancing your practice and the strength of your spell work. As you know, magical tools that you create for yourself are infused with your own unique energy and power, forging a bond between you and your instruments that will help increase the effectiveness of any rituals you perform. You will find that any handmade items will feel much more natural to use and will be perfectly suited to your needs and desires.

SOOTHE YOUR SOUL WITH HOMEMADE MASSAGE CANDLES

Making massage candles is very similar to making any other type of potted candle. I recommend using soy wax as it is so gentle on the skin. Soy is also nice and soft, so it melts easily and stays together in a puddle after melting and can be reused by thrifty crafters. It won't irritate your skin unless you have a soy allergy; if you have an allergy to soy, you can use beeswax instead, which is widely used. (For example, beeswax is in nearly every single Burt's Bees product.) The addition of the oils prevents it from hardening again and enables your skin to absorb it. Essential oils or cosmetic-grade fragrance oils are also added to create a soothing atmosphere. All soap-making fragrances, which are also soy candle safe, are perfect choices for scenting your massage candles. Try the basic directions below to make your first candle. For every three ounces of wax, you'll add one ounce of liquid oil and one-quarter ounce of fragrance. I suggest making two candles in four-ounce metal tins while you master this craft.

You will need these elements:

- 2 ounces sweet almond oil or vitamin E oil
- 6 ounces high quality soy wax
- ½ ounce essential oil
- 2 four-ounce metal tins
- 2 six-inch candle wicks

Steps:

1. Melt the soy wax and oil in a double boiler over simmering water.

2. Add the essential oils and stir gently to avoid bubbling or spilling.

3. Once the wax has cooled somewhat but is still melted enough to pour, place the wicks in your containers and pour the wax.

4. Allow several hours for the candles to set and harden.

5. Trim the wicks to one-quarter of an inch above the top of the candle, and they're ready to use.

Uplifting and Calming Essential Oils for Candle Making

Traditionally, these oils are considered to have emotional healing properties as well as simply smelling marvelous on your skin and in your home. Just burning candles scented with these oils will be magical!

Cedarwood oil has a woody and pleasant aroma and can also act as a natural sedative. Studies indicate it stimulates the production of melatonin, regulates sleep patterns, and brings a sense of serenity. A pre-sleep massage with cedarwood oil is truly therapeutic and will allow you to rest deeply and awaken refreshed and ready for anything.

Clary sage essential oil not only has a splendid smell, but has been shown in studies to positively influence the levels of the happiness-stimulating chemical dopamine in the brain. Perfect for uplifting the mood, clary sage helps to ease feelings of anxiety by calming the mind while boosting confidence and self-esteem.

Jasmine oil has been widely noted to be among the best at calming the nerves and overcoming stress. For centuries, jasmine oil has been used as a natural remedy for anxiety, melancholy, sleeplessness, and even low libido. Jasmine dissipates negativity and helps stimulate a return to positivity in life.

Lime essential oil, as you perhaps guessed, smells just like the real fruit, wonderfully fresh and citrusy. Lime works well to refresh and uplift the mood, and it is lightly invigorating, which can work wonders for those suffering from the stress of fatigue, grief, and a sad and heavy heart. Using this essential oil in a massage at any time of day will help you to see the bright side of life.

Rose oil is not just for romance, it is also highly effective for stimulating the mind and promoting a sense of peace, tranquility, and well-being. If someone is dealing with feelings of depression or worries or is just down in the dumps, rose oil in a massage candle will promote feelings of joy and hope.

Sandalwood essential oil supports mental clarity and the ability to focus. With a lightly sweet and woody scent, it is also supremely grounding. When you're dealing with the challenging demands of a hectic work schedule and long hours, taking time for a massage is essential for your overall well-being and mental health. Sandalwood essential oil offers balance along with feelings of harmony and inner peace.

CREATE STAINED-GLASS DECORATED CANDLES

To enhance the magic of your ritual candles, you can create your own, filling them with your energy and intentions! You can adorn them with big sequins, curio crosses, symbols such as the Egyptian ankh, faux pearls, or anything lovely and suitably glittery that can be added to the sides of the candles to create a "stained glass" appearance. Another technique is to mix in your magical objects, stirring them into the melted wax inside a mold. An even easier way to do this is to take a soft beeswax pillar candle and "stud" the sides and the candle top with tiny crystal pieces that cost just pennies per pound. You can save them after melting the candles down and reuse them again and again. Nowadays, candle-making classes abound, and you can get leftover or "recycled" wax to use, melt, and pour into glass votives for your own uniquely magical candle creations.

DO-IT-YOURSELF ALTAR CANDELABRA

Candelabras are an excellent addition to your altar to hold your ritual candles as well as to set the mood. Both elegant and romantic, with molten wax flowing down the sides, they can be nothing less than splendid. While you can always buy a candelabra, it is much better to make them yourself and place your imprimatur and your own special kind of magic in them. The following are the steps I learned from the one and only Aurelio Voltaire, who is a writer, musician, animator, graphic novelist, comic, and all-around Renaissance man.

Supplies:

- Empty wine bottles
- Black spray paint (or a color of your choice)
- Spray adhesive
- Paper images or stickers
- Candles

Directions:

1. Have fun by emptying some bottles of wine, preferably by drinking their contents! If you do not imbibe, you can get bottles from friends or from a recycling center.

2. Give the bottles a good spraying with the flat black paint and let them dry.

3. You can stop here, but it is even better to refine your design with your own art, stickers you particularly love, or even decoupaged (or spray-glued) photos evocative of your mood and magic. Voltaire recommends the "Bandelabra," featuring photos, stickers, lyrics, or

an image representing your favorite band, such as Dead Can Dance's beautiful images of hands and serpent coils from their CD covers, or a particularly spooky-looking shot of Siouxsie Sioux, of The Cure's Robert Smith, or maybe even of the beautiful and very talented Voltaire! Personally, I like to use still shots from movies that I feel reflect my personal pagan energy. Some examples for a dark pagan might be any and all Dracula movies, *The Rocky Horror Picture Show*, *The Crow*, *The Nightmare Before Christmas*, or *The Book of Life*. As long as these are for your own enjoyment and edification, you do not have to be concerned about copyrights, but if you suddenly decide to start eBaying your handcrafted candelabras, you must get legal clearance.

A personal favorite of mine is Francis Ford Coppola's *Bram Stoker's Dracula*; and above all, my favorite moment in this gorgeous visual feast is the absinthe-inspired section with verdant greens, light and shadow play, and yearning past-life romance. So, I suggest leaving the wine bottle in its native green state and going for green candles with a touch of green glitter and emerald stick-on stones to evoke the green fairy.

This is the easiest candelabrum of all—just place a candle inside the neck of the bottle, light it, and you have a very elegant and dreamy-looking light source.

IN CONCLUSION:

DESIGNING YOUR OWN RITUALS:
TRADITIONAL AND ALTERNATIVE

In this book are many examples of rituals, both traditional and alternative. In addition, there are ideas and suggestions for rituals of your own design. In creating your own rites and ceremonies, you can take many approaches. You can devise and enact new customs of your own invention. These new rituals can be pure, simple, uncomplicated events, or they can be incredibly elaborate. You decide. I urge you to avoid too much pomp. Too much planning, building, and painting of backdrops and excessive focus on research can create more stress than is really warranted, taking away from the meaning and distracting you from your true intention.

Participating in ritual can change your life. Even engaging in one ritual can uplift and inspire you for years, and regular involvement can lead to spiritual riches. Ritual is soul work. Increasingly, with our hectic workday schedules, you may find yourself creating rituals and meditating alone, praying by yourself, and performing daily spiritual practices solo. In addition to planning more intricate proceedings, you should also craft little on-the-spot private rituals that serve immediate spiritual needs. You can celebrate your gratitude to a deity that is special to you or light a candle and meditate at your altar on a holy day. Your rituals should reflect the ebb and flow of your outer life and your inner work.

This kind of ritual is simple and pure; I call it *real ritual*. Your spiritual pursuits should be a mix of simple solo ceremonies and more complex ones that you perform alone or with others. The work of the soul is stimulated by interactions with others and yet grows in your time alone. Rituals enliven and add meaning to each day. Your simple daily ceremonies and practices are the individual threads that weave the fabric of your life, rather like a tapestry quilt that grows thread by thread, stitch by stitch, and square by square. You need the threads, the patches, and the squares to hold together the tapestry of a rich, memory-filled, and meaningful life.

In this book, you have been provided with some of the great rituals of the world and many starting points for piecing together your own ceremonies. You can choose from the wealth of correspondences in the appendix to add layers of meaning, depth, and effectiveness, while building your knowledge, expanding your experiences, and connecting to the world's wise traditions. Also, by keeping a Book of Shadows or personal ritual journal, you will have your own set of measurements and memories of what has worked for you. The appendix gives ingredients that you can add to your ritual "recipe." Let's say you want to create a personal and private ritual to get a new job. You can look up the best time to do it in the Ritual Resources section, where you will see that a Thursday new moon would be an optimum choice to perform such a ritual.

There are different divinities you can choose to call upon for help in this ritual, from jovial Jupiter to the very sympathetic and helpful Lakshmi, to name just two. There are also a variety of herbs and plants you can decide to utilize to assist with money matters, along with correct colors for candles and essences for both incense and oils that supply abundance. When you create your new job ritual, therefore, you can select the right traditional correspondence that matches your need and you are halfway there.

Focus and attention concerning your intention are of equal importance. In terms of the language of your original ritual, you should write from your heart, which will ensure that the words will personally affect you and work for you. Believe in yourself and believe in your intention, and the right words will flow. There is no exact science to writing rituals. Just match the words and correspondences to your intention, and you will be a creator of rituals.

It is natural that once you are completely comfortable working with the realm of existing rituals, you should begin to trust your own intuition and create your own. Listen to your inner voice and trust yourself. Correspondences are a start, but you must take a leap of faith and delve into the depths of your own psyche for rituals you create, enact, and share with the world.

While we know there is no exact science to ritual design, there is an art to it, and the knack is developed from participating in group rituals, learning from experienced elders, performing private rituals, and endeavoring to craft rituals on your own for every season and reason. The art of creating rituals is work of the heart, and while it is not always easy, it is the work of creating joy in your life. With each ritual, you are taking a step to a reality of your own creation. Rites and ceremonies serve many purposes in our lives. They can be designed to fulfill one person's wish, help a member of your spiritual circle, or even help heal the entire world like the Dalai Lama's sand mandala ritual. There are no limitations to the scope of the rituals you can design. Where there is need, you can supply intention and inspiration, and in so doing, spread bliss in your wake. Rituals can change the world, and your rituals will most certainly change your world. When you are designing ritual, you are really designing the life of your dreams.

APPENDIX:

RITUAL RESOURCES

DATES AND TIMES

This section contains lists and tables of information you can use to cast spells and work magic using correspondences between dates, planets, goals, and astrological signs. (If a date is listed as being both lucky and unlucky, the ritualist is free to make his or her own decision regarding personal practice.)

Sabbats

FOUR MAJOR SABBATS:

1. **Candlemas**—February 2
2. **Beltane**—May 1
3. **Lammas**—August 1
4. **Samhain**—October 31

FOUR LESSER SABBATS:

1. **Vernal Equinox**—March 21
2. **Summer Solstice**—June 21
3. **Autumn Equinox**—September 21
4. **Winter Solstice/Yule**—December 21

Lucky and Unlucky Dates

MONTH: JANUARY
LUCKY DATES: 3, 10, 27, 31
UNLUCKY DATES: 12, 23

MONTH: FEBRUARY
LUCKY DATES: 7, 8, 18
UNLUCKY DATES: 2, 10, 17, 22

MONTH: MARCH
LUCKY DATES: 3, 9, 12, 14, 16
UNLUCKY DATES: 13, 19, 23, 28

MONTH: APRIL
LUCKY DATES: 5, 17
UNLUCKY DATES: 18, 20, 29, 30

MONTH: MAY
LUCKY DATES: 1, 2, 4, 6, 9, 14
UNLUCKY DATES: 10, 17, 20

MONTH: JUNE
LUCKY DATES: 3, 5, 7, 9, 13, 23
UNLUCKY DATES: 4, 20

MONTH: JULY
LUCKY DATES: 2, 6, 10, 23, 30
UNLUCKY DATES: 5, 13, 27

MONTH: AUGUST
LUCKY DATES: 5, 7, 10, 14
UNLUCKY DATES: 2, 13, 27, 31

MONTH: SEPTEMBER
LUCKY DATES: 6, 10, 13, 18, 30
UNLUCKY DATES: 13, 16, 18

MONTH: OCTOBER
LUCKY DATES: 13, 16, 25, 31
UNLUCKY DATES: 3, 9, 27

MONTH: NOVEMBER
LUCKY DATES: 1, 13, 23, 30
UNLUCKY DATES: 6, 25

MONTH: DECEMBER
LUCKY DATES: 10, 20, 29
UNLUCKY DATES: 15, 26

Days, Planets, Colors, and Goals

DAY: SUNDAY
PLANET: SUN
CORRESPONDENCES: EXORCISM, HEALING, PROSPERITY
COLOR: ORANGE, WHITE, YELLOW
INCENSE: LEMON, FRANKINCENSE

DAY: MONDAY
PLANET: MOON
CORRESPONDENCES: AGRICULTURE, ANIMALS, FEMALE
FERTILITY, MESSAGES, RECONCILIATION, VOYAGES
COLOR: SILVER, WHITE, GRAY
INCENSE: AFRICAN VIOLET, HONEYSUCKLE,
MYRTLE, WILLOW, WORMWOOD

DAY: TUESDAY
PLANET: MARS
CORRESPONDENCES: COURAGE, PHYSICAL STRENGTH, REVENGE,
MILITARY HONORS, SURGERY, BREAKING NEGATIVE SPELLS
COLOR: RED, ORANGE
INCENSE: DRAGON'S BLOOD, PATCHOULI

DAY: WEDNESDAY
PLANET: MERCURY
CORRESPONDENCES: KNOWLEDGE, COMMUNICATION,
DIVINATION, WRITING, BUSINESS TRANSACTIONS
COLOR: YELLOW, GRAY, VIOLET, ALL OPALESCENT HUES
INCENSE: JASMINE, LAVENDER, SWEET PEA

DAY: THURSDAY

PLANET: JUPITER

CORRESPONDENCES: LUCK, HEALTH, HAPPINESS, LEGAL
MATTERS, MALE FERTILITY, TREASURE, WEALTH, EMPLOYMENT

COLOR: PURPLE, INDIGO

INCENSE: CINNAMON, MUSK, NUTMEG, SAGE

DAY: FRIDAY

PLANET: VENUS

CORRESPONDENCES: LOVE, ROMANCE, MARRIAGE, SEXUAL
MATTERS, PHYSICAL BEAUTY, FRIENDSHIPS, PARTNERSHIPS

COLOR: PINK, GREEN, AQUA, CHARTREUSE

INCENSE: STRAWBERRY, ROSE, SANDALWOOD, SAFFRON, VANILLA

DAY: SATURDAY

PLANET: SATURN

CORRESPONDENCES: SPIRIT, COMMUNICATION, MEDITATION,
PSYCHIC ATTACK OR DEFENSE, LOCATING LOST OR MISSING PERSONS

COLOR: BLACK, GRAY, INDIGO

INCENSE: POPPY SEEDS, MYRRH

Sun Sign Correspondences

BIRTH DATE: MARCH 21 TO APRIL 19

SUN SIGN: ARIES

LUCKY AND PROTECTIVE STONES AND MINERALS:
DIAMOND, AMETHYST, TOPAZ, GARNET, IRON, STEEL

COLOR: RED

BIRTH DATE: APRIL 19 TO MAY 20

SUN SIGN: TAURUS

LUCKY AND PROTECTIVE STONES AND MINERALS: CORAL, SAPPHIRE, EMERALD, TURQUOISE, AGATE, ZIRCON, COPPER
COLOR: AZURE

BIRTH DATE: MAY 20 TO JUNE 21
SUN SIGN: GEMINI
LUCKY AND PROTECTIVE STONES AND MINERALS: AQUAMARINE, AGATE, AMBER, EMERALD, TOPAZ, ALUMINUM
COLOR: ELECTRIC BLUE

BIRTH DATE: JUNE 21 TO JULY 22
SUN SIGN: CANCER
LUCKY AND PROTECTIVE STONES AND MINERALS: OPAL, PEARL, EMERALD, MOONSTONE, SILVER
COLOR: PEARL OR ROSE

BIRTH DATE: JULY 22 TO AUGUST 22
SUN SIGN: LEO
LUCKY AND PROTECTIVE STONES AND MINERALS: DIAMOND, RUBY, GOLD, SARDONYX, CHRYSOBERYL
COLOR: ORANGE

BIRTH DATE: AUGUST 22 TO SEPTEMBER 23
SUN SIGN: VIRGO
LUCKY AND PROTECTIVE STONES AND MINERALS: JADE, RHODONITE, SAPPHIRE, CARNELIAN, ALUMINUM
COLOR: GRAY BLUE

BIRTH DATE: SEPTEMBER 23 TO OCTOBER 23
SUN SIGN: LIBRA
LUCKY AND PROTECTIVE STONES AND MINERALS: OPAL, SAPPHIRE, JADE, QUARTZ, TURQUOISE, COPPER
COLOR: PALE ORANGE

BIRTH DATE: OCTOBER 23 TO NOVEMBER 22

SUN SIGN: SCORPIO

LUCKY AND PROTECTIVE STONES AND MINERALS:
BLOODSTONE, TOPAZ, AQUAMARINE, JASPER, SILVER

COLOR: DARK RED

BIRTH DATE: NOVEMBER 22 TO DECEMBER 21

SUN SIGN: SAGITTARIUS

LUCKY AND PROTECTIVE STONES AND MINERALS:
LAPIS LAZULI, TOPAZ, TURQUOISE, CORAL, TIN

COLOR: PURPLE

BIRTH DATE: DECEMBER 21 TO JANUARY 20

SUN SIGN: CAPRICORN

LUCKY AND PROTECTIVE STONES AND MINERALS:
ONYX, JET, RUBY, LEAD, MALACHITE

COLOR: BROWN

BIRTH DATE: JANUARY 20 TO FEBRUARY 19

SUN SIGN: AQUARIUS

LUCKY AND PROTECTIVE STONES AND MINERALS:
AQUAMARINE, JADE, FLUORITE, SAPPHIRE, ZIRCON, AMETHYST

COLOR: GREEN

BIRTH DATE: FEBRUARY 19 TO MARCH 21

SUN SIGN: PISCES

LUCKY AND PROTECTIVE STONES AND MINERALS: AMETHYST,
ALEXANDRITE, BLOODSTONE, STITCHITE SERPENTINE, SILVER

COLOR: OCEAN BLUE

Daytime Planetary Hours

HOUR	SUN	MON	TUES	WED	THURS	FRI	SAT
1 6–7 a.m.	Sun	Moon	Mars	Mercury	Jupiter	Venus	Saturn
2 7–8 a.m.	Venus	Saturn	Sun	Moon	Mars	Mercury	Jupiter
3 8–9 a.m.	Mercury	Jupiter	Venus	Saturn	Sun	Moon	Mars
4 9–10 a.m.	Moon	Mars	Mercury	Jupiter	Venus	Saturn	Sun
5 10–11 a.m.	Saturn	Sun	Moon	Mars	Mercury	Jupiter	Venus
6 11–12 a.m.	Jupiter	Venus	Saturn	Sun	Moon	Mars	Mercury
7 12–1 p.m.	Mars	Mercury	Jupiter	Venus	Saturn	Sun	Moon
8 1–2 p.m.	Sun	Moon	Mars	Mercury	Jupiter	Venus	Saturn
9 2–3 p.m.	Venus	Saturn	Sun	Moon	Mars	Mercury	Jupiter
10 3–4 p.m.	Mercury	Jupiter	Venus	Saturn	Sun	Moon	Mars

11 4–5 p.m.	Moon	Mars	Mer- cury	Jupiter	Venus	Saturn	Sun
12 5–6 p.m.	Saturn	Sun	Moon	Mars	Mer- cury	Jupiter	Venus

Nighttime Planetary Hours

HOUR	SUN	MON	TUES	WED	THURS	FRI	SAT
1 6–7 p.m.	Jupiter	Venus	Saturn	Sun	Moon	Mars	Mer- cury
2 7–8 p.m.	Mars	Mer- cury	Jupiter	Venus	Saturn	Sun	Moon
3 8–9 p.m.	Sun	Moon	Mars	Mer- cury	Jupiter	Venus	Saturn
4 9–10 p.m.	Venus	Saturn	Sun	Moon	Mars	Mer- cury	Jupiter
5 10–11 p.m.	Mer- cury	Jupiter	Venus	Saturn	Sun	Moon	Mars
6 11–12 p.m.	Moon	Mars	Mer- cury	Jupiter	Venus	Saturn	Sun
7 12–1 a.m.	Saturn	Sun	Moon	Mars	Mer- cury	Jupiter	Venus
8 1–2 a.m.	Jupiter	Venus	Saturn	Sun	Moon	Mars	Mer- cury

9 2–3 a.m.	Mars	Mercury	Jupiter	Venus	Saturn	Sun	Moon
10 3–4 a.m.	Sun	Moon	Mars	Mercury	Jupiter	Venus	Saturn
11 4–5 a.m.	Venus	Saturn	Sun	Moon	Mars	Mercury	Jupiter
12 5–6 a.m.	Mercury	Jupiter	Venus	Saturn	Sun	Moon	Mars

Numbers

The following is based on the ancient Pythagorean system (on which modern-day numerology is also based). If any number keeps appearing to you in various forms, pay attention to the meanings for that number.

One: Independence, new beginnings, self-development, oneness with life, individuality, progress, and creativity

Two: A balance of the yin and yang energies (the polarities) of the universe, self-surrender, putting others first, a dynamic attraction to one another, knowledge that comes from balancing the two opposites

Three: Trinity, mind-body-spirit, threefold nature of divinity, expansion, expression, communication, fun, self-expression, giving outwardly, openness and optimism (this number relates to the Wiccan three-by-three law of returns—whatever you send out, you will receive threefold)

Four: Security, foundations, the four elements and the four directions, self-discipline through work and service, productivity, organization, wholeness

Five: Feeling free, self-emancipation, active, physical, impulsive, energetic, changing, adventuresome, resourceful, travel, curiosity, free soul, excitement, change

Six: Self-harmony, compassion, love, service, social responsibility, beauty, the arts, generosity, concern, caring, children, balance, community service

Seven: Inner life and inner wisdom, seven chakras and seven heavens, birth and rebirth, religious strength, sacred vows, path of solitude, analysis, contemplation

Eight: Infinity, material prosperity, self-power, abundance, cosmic consciousness, reward, authority, leadership

Nine: Humanitarianism, selflessness, dedication of your life to others, completion, endings, universal compassion, tolerance, and wisdom

Master Numbers

In the Pythagorean tradition, master numbers were thought to have a special power and significance of their own.

Eleven: Developing intuition, clairvoyance, spiritual healing, and other metaphysical faculties

Twenty-two: Unlimited potential of mastery in any area—spiritual, physical, emotional, and mental

Thirty-Three: All things are possible

A Full Moon by Any Other Name

Many of our full moon names come from medieval books of hours as well as from North American indigenous traditions. Here are other, rarer names from these two traditions that you may want to use in your lunar rituals.

- **January:** Old Moon, Chaste Moon
- **February:** Hunger Moon
- **March:** Crust Moon, Sugar Moon, Sap Moon, or Worm Moon
- **April:** Sprouting Grass Moon, Egg Moon, Fish Moon
- **May:** Milk Moon, Corn Planting Moon, Dyad Moon
- **June:** Hot Moon, Rose Moon
- **July:** Buck Moon, Hay Moon
- **August:** Barley Moon, Wort Moon, Sturgeon Moon
- **September:** Green Corn Moon, Wine Moon
- **October:** Dying Grass Moon, Travel Moon, Blood Moon, Moon of Changing Seasons
- **November:** Frost Moon, Snow Moon
- **December:** Cold Moon, Oak Moon

Saturn's Return

The rhythm of the planets in each of our charts is also a determining factor. One astrological factor that determines when a woman becomes a crone is when she reaches her second Saturn Return, which is when Saturn returns for the second time to the place it occupied when she was born. Usually, this occurs sometime between the ages of fifty-four and fifty-eight. Because Saturn is the planet of wisdom, it is also a "teaching planet." Saturn moves slowly and gives us all time to grow into our wisdom. A good astrological natal chart can teach you a great deal about yourself.

GOD AND SPIRIT CORRESPONDENCES

The following lists and tables contain information on magical goals and their related deities. If you wish to work with particular deities, include images or objects sacred to them on your altar and consider calling upon them in your rituals.

Deities and Their Domains

Agriculture: Adonis, Amon, Aristaeus, Baldur, Bonus Eventus, Ceres, Consus, Dagon, Demeter, Dumuzi, Esus, Gahanan, Inari, Osiris, Saturn, Tammuz, Thor, Triptolemus, Vertumnus, Yumcaa, Zochipilli

Arts: Athena, Ea, Hathor, Odin, Thor

Astrology: Urania

Cats: Bast, Sekhmet, Freya

Childbirth: Althea, Anahita, Bes, Carmenta, Cihuatcoatl, Cuchavira, Isis, Kuan Yin, Laima, Lucina, Meshkent

Communications: Hermes, Janus, Mercury

Courage: Tyr

Dreams: Geshtinanna, Morpheus, Nanshe

Earth: Asia, Consus, Dagda, Enlil, Frigga, Gaea, Ge, Geb, Kronos, Ninhursag, Ops, Prithivi, Rhea, Saturn, Sif, Tellus

Fertility: Amnu, Anaitis, Apollo, Arianrhod, Asherali, Astarte, Attis, Baal, Bacchus, Bast, Bona Dea, Boucca, Centeotle, Cernunnos, Cerridwen,

Cybele, Dagda, Demeter, Dew, Dionysus, Eostre, Frey, Freya, Frigg, Indra, Ishtar, Ishwara, Isis, Kronos, Ono, Lupercus, Min, Mut, Mylitta, Ningirsu, Ops, Osiris, Ostara, Pan, Pomona, Quetzalcoatl, Rhea, Rhiannon, Saturn, Selkhet, Sida, Tane, Telepinu, Telluno, Tellus Mater, Thunor, Tlazolteotl, Yarilo, Zarpanitu

Good Luck and Fortune: Bonus Eventus, Daikoku, Fortuna, Ganesha, Jorojin, Laima, Tyche

Healing: Apollo, Asclepius, Bast, Brigid, Eir, Gula, Ixlilton, Khnos, Paeon, Quan Yin

Journeys: Echua, Janus

Law, Truth, and Justice: Astraea, Maat, Misharu, Themis

Love: Aizen, Myo-O, Alpan, Angus Óg, Aphrodite, Ashera, Astarte, Ashtoreth, Belili, Creirwy, Cupid, Dzydzilelya, Eros, Erzulie, Esmeralda, Fenrua, Freya, Frigg, Habondia, Hathor, Inanna, Ishtar, Kades, Kama, Kivan-Non, Kubaba, Melusine, Menu, Minne, Mamaja, Odudua, Olwen, Oshun, Prenda, Rao, Sauska, Tlazoletotl, Turan, Venus, Xochipilli, Zochiquetzal

Lunar Magic: Aah, Anahita, Artemis, Asherali, Astarte, Baiame, Bendis, Diana, Gou, Hathor, Hecate, Ilmaqah, Ishtar, Isis, Jacy, Kabul, Khons, Kilya, Lucina, Luna, Mah, Mama Quilla, Mani, Menu, Metzli, Myestaa, Nanna, Pah, Selene, Sin, Soma, Taukiyomi, Thoth, Varuna, Yarikh, Yerak, Zamna

Marriage: Airyaman, Aphrodite, Bes, Bah, Ceres, Errata, Frigg, Hathor, Hera, Hymen, Juno, Patina, Saluki, Svarog, Thalassa, Tutunis, Vor, Xochipilli

Music and/or Poetry: Apollo, Benten, Bragi, Brigid, Hathor, Odin, Orpheus, Thoth, Untunktahe, Woden, Xolotl

Reincarnation: Hera, Khensu, Ra

Sea: Amphitrite, Benten, Dylan, Ea, Enoil, Glaucus, Leucothea, Manannan Mac Lir, Mariamne, Neptune, Nereus, Njord, Paldemon, Phorcys, Pontus, Poseidon, Proteus, Shoney, Yamm, Yemaya

Shapeshifting: Freya, Nerthus, Volkh, Xolotl

Sky: Aditi, Anshar, Anu, Dyaus, Frigg, Hathor, Horus, Joch-Huva, Jupiter, Kumarbis, Nut, Obatala, Rangi, Svarog, Tane, Thor, Tiwaz, Ukko, Uranus, Varuna, Zeus

Sleep: Hypnos (also see the list of deities who rule over dreams)

Solar Magic: Amaterasu, Apollo, Atum, Baldur, Bochia, Dazhbog, Helios, Hiruku, Horus, Hyperion, Inti, Legba, Lugh, Mandulis, Mao, Marduk, Maui, Melkart, Mithra, Orunjan, Paiva Perun, Phoebus, Ra, Sabazius, Samas, Sams, Shamash, Sol, Sunna, Surya, Texcatlipoca, Tonatiuh, Torushompek, Utto, Vishnu, Yhi

Vengeance: Nemesis

Wealth and Prosperity: Daikoku, Jambhala, Kuber, Lakshmi, Plutus, Thor

Weatherworking: Adad, Acolus, Agni, Amen, Baal, Bragi, Burlash, Catequil, Chac-Mool, Chernabog, Donar, Fomagata, Ilyapa, Indra, Jove, Jupiter, Kami-Nari, Koza, Lei-Kung, Marduk, Nyame, Oya, Perkunas, Pillan, Pulug, Quiateot, Raiden, Rammon, Rudra, Shango, Sobo, Summanus, Taki-Tsu-Hilo, Tawhaaki, Tawhiri, Tefnut, Thor, Thunor, Tilo, Tinia, Typhoeus, Typhon, Yu-Tzu, Zeus, Zu

Wisdom: Aruna, Athena, Atri, Baldur, Brigid, Dainichi, Ea, Enki, Fudo-Myoo, Fugen Bosatsu, Fukurokuju, Ganesha, Hecate, Minerva, Nebo, Mimir, Oannes, Odin, Oghama, Quetzalxoatl, Sia, Sin, Thoth, Vohumano, Zeus

Magical Intentions

The following words correspond to various planets and elements. See below to learn more.

Banishing: Saturn, fire

Beauty: Venus, water

Courage: Mars, fire

Divination: Mercury, air

Employment: Sun, Jupiter

Energy: Sun, Mars, fire

Exorcism: Sun, fire

Fertility: Moon, planet earth

Friendship: Venus, water

Happiness: Venus, Moon, water

Healing and Health: Moon, Mars (to burn away disease), fire (the same), water

Home: Saturn, Earth, water

Joy and Happiness: Venus, water

Love: Venus, water

Money and Wealth: Jupiter, Earth

Peace: Moon, Venus

Power: Sun, Mars, fire

Protection: Sun, Mars, fire

Psychism: Moon, water

Sex: Mars, Venus, fire

Sleep: Moon, water

Spirituality: Sun, Moon

Success: Sun, fire

Travel: Mercury

Wisdom and Intelligence: Mercury, air

Elemental Dragons

ELEMENT	MANIFESTATION	CARDINAL POINTS	DRAGON NAME	COLOR
Earth	Land and Moonbeams	North	Grael	Clear Dark Green
Water	Oceans and Rivers	West	Naelyan	Blue
Air	Breezes and Wind	East	Sairys	Yellow
Fire	Sunbeams	South	Fafnir	Pure Red
Light Side of the Soul	Mother	N/A	N/A	White
Dark Side of the Soul	Father	N/A	N/A	Black

Elemental Spirits

ELEMENT	SPIRIT NAME	LEADER	ATTRACTED BY	RULERS OF
Earth	Gnomes or Trolls	Ghob	Salts and Powders	Riches and Treasure
Water	Nymphs or Undines	Neckna	Washes and Solutions	Plants and Healings
Air	Sylphs or Zephyrs	Paralda	Oils and Incense	Knowledge and Inspiration
Fire	Salamanders	Dijn	Fire and Incense	Freedom and Change

Wild Women

For your celebratory mask-making ceremonies, you can and should design your own wild woman images. You can also choose from a list of classical goddess images, such as:

- Peacock Woman is **Juno**, whose totem is the royally plumed bird
- **Winged Isis** wears the sun disk on her head
- **Medusa** has snakes for hair
- **The Sphinx** is an image of eternal mystery
- **Saints** are holy women with halos
- **Mermaid goddesses** wear tricorn crowns
- **Imps** and some underworld goddesses have horns
- **Diana** has the crescent moon on her head
- **Fairies** at times have butterfly-like wings and antennae
- **Elves** have pointed ears
- **Dryads** are tree nymphs with leafy crowns
- **Anima Mundi**, the "soul of the world," has a crown of stars

HERBS OF THE GODS AND GODDESSES

Herbs are a very direct way to connect to different divinities. You can use these energies in so many ways—gardens, potpourris, incenses, and teas. Always check with your physician, an herbalist, or an appropriate specialist, before using them in anything you plan to ingest. Caution is always your best guide in herbology.

Acacia: Buddha, Neith, and Osiris

Aconite: Hecate and Medea **(warning: toxic)**

Agave: Mayauel (Aztec goddess of birth and death)

All Heal: Hercules

Anemone: Venus and Adonis

Angelica: Archangel Michael

Anise: Mercury and Apollo

Azalea: Hecate

Barley: Odin, John Barleycorn (the Green Man)

Basil: Lakshmi, Krishna, Vishnu, Erzulie (Haitian goddess of love)

Belladonna: Bellona, Circe, Hecate, Atropos (the fate who cuts the thread) **(warning: toxic)**

Benzoin: Venus and Nut (Egyptian vulture goddess and patroness of Thebes)

Blackthorn: The Triple Goddess

Broom: Blodeuwedd (Welsh goddess of spring)

Catnip: Bast (Egyptian cat goddess) and Sekhmet (Egyptian lion-headed sun goddess)

Centaury: Chiron

Chamomile: Karnaya

Coltsfoot: Epona

Cornflower: Flora

Cowslip: Freya

Crocus: Venus

Daffodil: Persephone

Daisy: Artemis, Freya, Thor, Venus, and Zeus

Dandelion: Brigid

Dittany: Consus (Roman god of grain storage and secret councils)

Elecampane: Helen

Eyebright: Euphrosyne (Greek goddess of mirth, one of the Charities)

Fennel: Adonis

Fenugreek: Apollo

Ferns: Kupala (Polish water and mother goddess of the summer solstice, herbs, trees, and sex)

Flax: Hulda (Teutonic fertility goddess)

Garlic: Mars and Hecate

Hawthorn: Hymen

Heather: Venus and Isis

Heliotrope: Apollo, Sol, Ra, and Helios

Holly: Frau Holle (Scandinavian goddess of healing)

Horehound: Horus

Hyacinth: Artemis, Apollo, and Hyacinthus

Iris: Isis, Hera, and Iris

Ivy: Dionysus, Osiris, Attis

Jasmine: Diana

Jimsonweed: Apollo, Kwawar (Great Spirit and Creator of the Gabrielino Indians)

Lady's Mantle: Benevolent Virgin Mary

Lavender: Hecate, Hestia, and Cronos

Leek: Thor and Jupiter

Lettuce: Adonis

Lily: Lilith, Ostara, Hera, and Astarte

Lotus: Kuan Yin, Lakshmi, Osiris, Tara, Buddha, Brahma, Isis, Horus, Mercury

Maidenhair Fern: Venus, Dis, and Kupala

Mandrake: Hecate, Venus, Cronos, and Circe

Marigold: Xochiquetzal (Aztec goddess of love, earth, flowers, dance, and games)

Marjoram: Venus

Meadowsweet: Blodeuwedd

Mints: Mintha, Hecate, and Dis (Norse goddess of the Disablot, a midwinter drinking festival)

Mistletoe: Zeus, Odin, and Aeneas

Monkshood: Hecate, Cerberus (Hellhound of the Greek Underworld) **(warning: toxic)**

Moonwort: Selene, Thoth, Diana, Artemis

Mosses: Tapio (Finnish forest god)

Motherwort: All mother goddesses

Mugwort: Artemis, Diana

Mulberry: Athena

Mullein: Odysseus and Circe

Narcissus: Narcissus, Venus, Dis, Hades, and Persephone

Orchid: Bacchus and Orcus

Orris root: Venus, Juno, Iris, Isis, and Osiris

Osier: Hecate

Parsley: Venus, Persephone

Pennyroyal: Demeter

Peppermint: Zeus

Periwinkle: Venus

Plantain: Venus

Poppy: Diana, Persephone, and Ceres

Primrose: Freya

Purslane: Hermes

Raspberry: Venus

Reeds: Pan, Inanna

Rose: Cupid, Venus, Demeter, Erato, Eros, Flora, Freya, Hathor, Holda, the Virgin Mary

Rue: Mars

Rush: Acis (Greek river deity)

Rye: Ceres

Sage: Consus and Zeus

Sandalwood: Venus

Saxifrage: Kupala

Solomon's Seal: King Solomon

Strawberry: Venus, Freya, Virgin Mary

Sugar Cane: Kama, Eros

Sunflower: Apollo, Demeter, Sol, Mary

Tansy: Ganymede (cupbearer of Zeus)

Tarragon: Lilith

Thistle: Thor

Trefoil: Olwen

Verbena: Diana

Vervain: Cerridwen, Demeter, Diana, Hermes, Isis, Thor, Mars, Jupiter, Juno, Hermes, Aradia (Italian goddess of the magical arts)

Violet: Venus, Attis, Zeus, and Io (Greek maiden and lover of Zeus)

Water Lily: All water deities, Surya (Indian fire god and/or goddess)

Wood Sorrel: St. Patrick

Wormwood: Diana

Yarrow: Achilles and the Horned God

The Language of Flowers

Here is what each of the following flowers means so that you can select the right flowers for your ritual.

A

Abatina: Fickleness

Acacia: Chaste love

Acacia, Pink: Elegance

Acacia, Yellow: Secret love

Acanthus: The fine arts, artifice

Achillea Millefolia: War

Aconite, Crowfoot: Lustre

Aconite, Wolfsbane: Misanthropy

Adonis: Sorrowful remembrance

African Marigold: Vulgar minds

Agnus Castus: Coldness

Agrimony: Gratitude, thankfulness

Almond: Stupidity, indiscretion

Almond, Flowering: Hope

Almond, Laurel: Perfidy

Allspice: Compassion

Aloe: Grief, affection

Althea Frutex: Persuasion

Alyssum, Sweet: Worth beyond beauty

Amaranth: Immortality, unfading love

Amaranth, Cockscomb: Foppery, affectation

Amaranth, Globe: Unchangeable

Amaryllis: Pride

Ambrosia: Love returned

American Elm: Patriotism

American Linden: Matrimony

B

Bachelor's Buttons: Single blessedness

Balm: Sympathy

Balm, Gentle: Pleasantry

Balm of Gilead: Cure, relief

Balsam: Impatience

Balsam, Red: Touch me not, impatient resolve

Barberry: Sourness, sharpness, ill temper

Basil: Hatred

Bay Leaf: I change but in death

Bay Tree: Glory

Bay Wreath: Reward of merit

Bearded Crepis: Protection

Bee Ophrys: Error

Bee Orchis: Industry

Beech Tree: Prosperity

Begonia: Dark thoughts

Bell Flower, White: I declare against you

Belladonna: Silence

Betony: Surprise

Bilberry: Treachery

Bindweed, Great: Insinuation

Bindweed, Small: Humility

Birch: Meekness

Birdsfoot Trefoil: Revenge

Bitterweed, Nightshade: Truth

Black Poplar: Courage

C

Cabbage: Profit

Cacalia: Adulation

Calceolaria: Keep this for my sake

Calla Aethiopica: Magnificent beauty

Calycanthus: Benevolence

Camellia Japonica, White: Unpretending excellence

Campanula: Gratitude

Canariensis: Self-esteem

Canary Grass: Perseverance

Candytuft: Indifference

Canterbury Bell: Acknowledgement

Cardamine: Paternal error

Cardinal Flower: Distinction

Carnation, Red: Alas for my poor heart

Carnation, Striped: Refusal

Carnation, Yellow: Disdain

Catchfly: Snare

Catchfly, Red: Youthful love

Catchfly, White: Betrayal

Catsus: Warmth

Cedar: Strength

Cedar of Lebanon: Incorruptible

Cedar Leaf: I live for thee

Celandine: Joys to come

Centuary: Felicity

Cerebus, Creeping:
Modest genius

Chamomile: Energy in adversity

Champignon: Suspicion

Crown, Imperial:
Majesty, powerful

D, E

Daffodil: Regard

Daffodil, Great Yellow: Chivalry

Dahlia: Instability

Dahlia, Single: Good taste

Daisy, Double: Participation

Daisy, Garden: I share
your sentiment

Daisy, One-Eyed: A token

Daisy, Parti-colored: Beauty

Daisy, Red: Unconscious

Daisy, White: Innocent

Daisy, Wild: I will think of it

Dandelion: Oracle

Daphne Odora: Painting the lily

Darnel: Vice

Dead Leaves: Sadness,
melancholy

Dew Plant: A serenade

Diosma: Uselessness

Dittany, White: Passion

Dittany of Crete: Birth

Dock: Patience

Dodder of Thyme: Baseness

Dogsbane: Deceit, falsehood

Dogwood: Durability

Dragon Plant: Snare

Dragonwort: Horror

Ebony Tree: Blackness

Eglantine or Sweet Briar:
Poetry; I wound to heal

Elder: Zealousness

Elm: Dignity

Enchanter's Nightshade:
Fascination, witchcraft

Endive: Frugality

Eschscholtzia: Sweetness

Eupatorium: Delay

Evergreen: Poverty

Evergreen, Thorn: Solace in adversity

Everlasting Pea: Lasting pleasure, an appointed meeting

F, G

Fennel: Worthy of all praise

Fern: Sincerity

Fern, Flowering: Fascination

Ficoides, Ice Plant: Your looks freeze me

Fig: Argument

Fig, Marigold: Idleness

Fig Tree: Prolific

Flax: Fate, domestic industry, I feel your kindness

Flax, Dried: Utility

Flax-leaved Golden Locks: Tardiness

Fleur-de-lis: Flame

Fleur-de-Luce: Confidence in heaven

Flower-of-an-Hour: Delicate beauty

Fly Orchis: Error

Fly Trap: Deceit

Fool's Parsley: Silliness

Forget-Me-Not: True love

Foxglove: Insincerity

Foxtail Grass: Sporting

French Honeysuckle: Rustic beauty

French Marigold: Jealousy

Fritillary, Checquered: Persecution

Frog Ophrys: Disgust

Fullers Teasel: Misanthropy, importunity

Fumitory: Spleen

Furze or Gorse: Enduring affection

Fuschia, Scarlet: Taste

Garden Anemone: Forsaken

Garden Chervil: Sincerity

Garden Marigold: Uneasiness

Garden Ranunculus: You are rich in attractions

Garden Sage: Esteem

Garland of Roses: Reward of virtue

Gentian: You are unjust

Geranium, Dark: Melancholy

Geranium, Ivy: Bridal favor

Geranium, Nutmeg: An expected meeting

Geranium, Oak-leaved: True friendship

Geranium, Pencil-leaved: Ingenuity

Geranium, Rose or Pink: Preference

Geranium, Scarlet: Comforting

Geranium, Silver-leaved: Recall

Geranium, Wild: Steadfast piety

Germander Speedwell: Facility

Gillyflower: Lasting beauty

Gladiolus: Strength of character

Glory Flower: Glorious beauty

Gloxinia: A proud spirit

Goat's Rue: Reason

H, I, J

Hand Flower Tree: Warming

Harebell: Submission, grief

Hawkweed: Quick sightedness

Hawthorne: Hope

Hazel: Reconciliation

Heartsease or Pansy: You occupy my thoughts

Heath: Solitude

Helenium: Tears

Heliotrope: Devotion

Hellebore: Scandal, calumny

Hemlock: You will be my death

Hemp: Fate

Henbane: Imperfection

Hepatica: Confidence

Hibiscus: Delicate beauty

Holly: Foresight

Holly Herb: Enchantment

Hollyhock: Fecundity

Honesty: Honesty, sincerity

Honey Flower: Love sweet and secret

Honeysuckle: Bonds of love, sweetness of disposition

Honeysuckle, Coral: The color of my fate

Honeysuckle, French: Rustic beauty

Hop: Injustice

Hornbeam: Ornament

Hortensia: You are cold

Houseleek: Vivacity, domestic economy

Houstonia: Content

Hoya: Sculpture

Humble Plant: Despotism

Hyacinth: Sport, game, play

Hyacinth, Blue: Constancy

Hyacinth, Purple: Sorrow

Hyacinth, White: Unobtrusiveness, loveliness

Hydrangea: A boaster, heartlessness

Hyssop: Cleanliness

Ice Plant: Your looks freeze me

Iceland Moss: Health

Imperial Montaque: Power

Indian Cress: Warlike trophy

Indian Pink, Double: Always lovely

Indian Plum: Privation

Iris: Message

Iris, German: Flame

Ivy: Friendship, fidelity

Ivy, Sprig of with tendrils: Assiduous to please

Jacob's Ladder: Come down

Japan Rose: Beauty is your only attraction

Jasmine, Cape: Transport of joy

Jasmine, Carolina: Separation

Jasmine, Indian: Attachment

Jasmine, Spanish: Sensuality

Jasmine, Yellow: Grace and elegance

Jasmine, White: Amiability

Jonquil: I desire a return of affection

Judas Tree: Unbelief, betrayal

Justicia: The perfection of female loveliness

K, L

Kennedya: Mental beauty

King-Cups: Desire of riches

Laburnum: Forsaken, pensive beauty

Lady's Slipper: Capricious beauty

Lagerstromia, Indian: Eloquence

Lantana: Rigor

Larch: Audacity, boldness

Larkspur: Lightness, levity

Larkspur, Pink: Fickleness

Larkspur, Purple: Haughtiness

Laurel: Glory

Laurel, Common in the flower: Perfidy

Laurel, Ground: Perseverance

Laurel, Mountain: Ambition

Laurestina: A token

Lavender: Distrust

Lemon: Zest

Lemon Blossoms: Fidelity in love

Lent Lilly: Sweet disposition

Lettuce: Cold-heartedness

Lichen: Dejection, solitude

Lilac, Field: Humility

Lilac, Purple: First emotions of love

Lilac, White: Youthful innocence

Lily, Day: Coquetry

Lily, Yellow: Falsehood, gaiety

Lily of the Valley: Return of happiness

Linden or Lime Tree: Conjugal love

Lint: I feel my obligation

Liquorice, Wild: I declare against you

Live Oak: Liberty

Liverwort: Confidence

Lobelia: Malevolence

Locust Tree: Elegance

Locust Tree, Green: Affection beyond the grave

London Pride: Frivolity

Lote Tree: Concord

Lotus: Eloquence

Lotus Flower: Estranged love

Lotus Leaf: Recantation

Love-in-a-Mist: Perplexity

Love-Lies-Bleeding: Hopeless, not heartless

Lucerne: Life

Lupin: Voraciousness

M, N, O

Madder: Calumny

Magnolia: Love of nature

Magnolia, Laurel-leaved: Dignity

Magnolia, Swamp: Perseverance

Mallow: Mildness

Mallow, Marsh: Beneficence

Mallow, Syrian: Consumed by love

Mallow, Venetian: Delicate beauty

Manchineel Tree: Falsehood

Mandrake: Horror

Maple: Reserve

Marigold: Grief, despair

Marigold, African: Vulgar minds

Marigold, French: Jealousy

Marigold, Prophetic: Prediction

Marjoram: Blushes

Marvel of Peru: Timidity

Meadow Lychnis: Wit

Meadow Saffron: My best days are past

Meadowsweet: Uselessness

Mercury: Goodness

Mesembryanthemum: Idleness

Mezereon: Desire to please

Michaelmas Daisy: Afterthought

Mignonette: Your qualities surpass your charms

Milfoil: War

Milkvetch: Your presence softens my pains

Milkwort: Hermitage

Mimosa, Sensitive Plant: Sensitivity

Mint: Virtue

Mistletoe: I surmount difficulties

Narcissus: Egotism

Narcissus, Double: Female ambition

Nasturtium: Patriotism

Nemophila: I forgive you

Nettle, Burning: Slander

Nettle, Common Stinging:
You are cruel

Night Convolvulus: Night

Night-blooming Cereus:
Transient beauty

Nightshade: Falsehood

Oak Leaves: Bravery

Oak Tree: Hospitality

Oats: The witching soul of music

Oleander: Beware

Olive: Peace

Orange Blossoms: Bridal
festivities; your purity equals
your loveliness

Orange Flowers: Chastity

Orange Tree: Generosity

Orchid: A belle

Osier: Frankness

Osmunda: Dreams

Ox Eye: Patience

P, Q, R

Palm: Victory

Pansy: Thoughts

Parsley: Festivity

Pasque Flower: You
have no claims

Passionflower:
Religious superstition

Patience Dock: Patience

Pea, Everlasting: An appointed
meeting, lasting pleasure

Pea, Sweet: Departure,
lasting pleasures

Peach: Your qualities are like your
charms unequalled

Peach Blossom: I am your captive

Quaking Grass: Agitation

Quamoclit: Busybody

Queen's Rocket: You are the
Queen of Coquettes, passion

Quince: Temptation

Ragged Robin: Wit

Ranunculus: You are radiant
with charms

Ranunculus, Garden: You are rich in all relations

Ranunculus, Wild: Ingratitude

Raspberry: Remorse

Red Catchfly: Youthful love

Reed: Complaisance, music

Reed, Split: Indiscretion

Rhododendron, Rosebay: Danger, beware

Rhubarb: Advice

Rocket: Rivalry

Rye Grass, Darnel: Vice

S

Saffron: Beware of success

Saffron, Crocus: Mirth

Saffron, Meadow: My happiest days are past

Sage: Domestic virtue

Sage, Garden: Esteem

Sainfoin: Agitation

Saint John's Wort: Animosity

Salvia, Blue: I think of you

Salvia, Red: Forever thine

Saxifrage, Mossy: Affection

Scabicus: Unfortunate love

Scarlet Lychnis: Sunbeaming eyes

Schinus: Religious enthusiasm

Scilla, Blue: Forgive and forget

Scilla, Sibirica: Pleasure without alloy

Scilla, White: Sweet innocence

Scotch Fir: Elevation

Sensitive Plant: Sensibility

Shamrock: Light-heartedness

Snakesfoot: Horror

Snowball: Bound

Snowdragon: Presumption

Snowdrop: Hope

Sorrel: Affection

Sorrel, Wild: Wit, ill-timed

Sorrel, Wood: Joy

Stephanotis: You can boast too much

Stock, Ten Week: Promptness

Stonecrop: Tranquility

Straw, Broken: Rupture of a contract

Straw, Whole: Union

Strawberry Blossom: Foresight

Strawberry Tree: Esteem, not love

Sumach, Venice (Smoke Tree): Splendor

Sunflower, Dwarf: Adoration

Sunflower, Tall: Haughtiness

T

Tamarisk: Crime

Tansy, Wild: I declare war against you

Teasel: Misanthropy

Tendrils of Climbing Plants: Ties

Thistle, Common: Austerity

Thistle, Scotch: Retaliation

Thorn Apple: Deceitful, charms

Thorns, Branch of: Severity

Thrift: Sympathy

Throatwort: Neglected beauty

Thyme: Activity

Tiger Flower: For once may pride befriend me

Traveler's Joy: Safety

Tree of Life: Old age

Trefoil: Revenge

Tremella: Resistance

Trillium Pictum: Modest beauty

Truffle: Surprise

Tulip, Red: Declaration of love

Tulip, Variegated: Beautiful eyes

Tulip, Yellow: Hopeless love

Turnip: Charity

Tussilago, Sweet-scented: Justice shall be done you

V, W

Valerian: An accommodating disposition

Valerian, Greek: Rupture

Venus Trap: Deceit

Venus's Car: Fly with me

Venus's Looking Glass: Flattery

Verbena, Scarlet: Sensibility

Verbena, White: Pure and guileless

Vernal Grass: Poor, but happy

Veronica: Fidelity

Vervain: Enchantment

Vine: Intoxication

Violet, Blue: Faithfulness

Violet, Dame: Watchfulness

Violet, Sweet: Modesty

Violet, Yellow: Rural happiness

Virgin's Bower: Filial love

Virginia Creeper: Ever changing

Volkmannia: May you be happy

Wallflower: Fidelity in adversity

Walnut: Intellect, stratagem

Water Lily: Purity of heart

Watermelon: Bulkiness

Wax Plant: Susceptibility

Weigela: Accept a faithful heart

Wheat Stalk: Riches

Whin: Anger

White Jasmine: Amiability

White Lily: Purity and modesty

White Mullein: Good nature

White Oak: Independent

Whortleberry: Treason

Willow, Creeping: Love forsaken

Willow, French: Bravery, humanity

Willow, Herb: Pretension

Willow, Water: Freedom

Willow, Weeping: Mourning

Wisteria: I cling to thee

Witch Hazel: A spell

Woodbine: Fraternal love

X, Y, Z

Xanthium: Rudeness, pertinacity

Xeranthemum: Cheerfulness under adversity

Yew: Sorrow

Zephyr Flower: Expectation

Zinnia: Thoughts of absent friends

ABOUT THE AUTHOR

Cerridwen Greenleaf has worked with many leading lights of the Wiccan world and has led ritual and magic workshops throughout North America. She is the author of *The Magic of Crystals and Gems* and *The Herbal Healing Handbook*. She blogs at yourmagicalhome.blogspot.com and lives in San Francisco, California.

Mango Publishing, established in 2014, publishes an eclectic list of books by diverse authors—both new and established voices—on topics ranging from business, personal growth, women's empowerment, LGBTQ studies, health, and spirituality to history, popular culture, time management, decluttering, lifestyle, mental wellness, aging, and sustainable living. We were recently named 2019 *and* 2020's #1 fastest-growing independent publisher by *Publishers Weekly.* Our success is driven by our main goal, which is to publish high-quality books that will entertain readers as well as make a positive difference in their lives.

Our readers are our most important resource; we value your input, suggestions, and ideas. We'd love to hear from you—after all, we are publishing books for you!

Please stay in touch with us and follow us at:

Facebook: Mango Publishing

Twitter: @MangoPublishing

Instagram: @MangoPublishing

LinkedIn: Mango Publishing

Pinterest: Mango Publishing

Newsletter: mangopublishinggroup.com/newsletter

Join us on Mango's journey to reinvent publishing, one book at a time.